THE CHILWI

A NEW INVESTIGATION

by

A R Dance

ARUNDEL
BOOKS

First published in Great Britain by the author in 1998
Reprinted 1999 and 2000

This version first published 2011 by
Arundel Books, 2, Audon Avenue, Chilwell,
Nottingham, NG9 4AW

Reprinted 2012 & 2013

www.arundelbooks.co.uk

ISBN 978-0-9558133-2-0

Typeset in Times New Roman 10pt, 11pt & 12pt

Printed and bound in Great Britain by
Russell Press, Basford, Nottingham

Further copies of this book can be purchased direct from the publisher
Post-free in the UK
Please send cheques payable to Arundel Books

CONTENTS

Acknowledgments
Introduction

ILLUSTRATIONS AND PHOTOGRAPHS

Acknowledgements

My thanks are due to the following individuals and organisations who have provided material or assisted in the production of this book, or given permission for the reproduction of illustrations and documents. The source is acknowledged at the foot of each plate.

Mr Steve Dance; Mr Roy Davies; Mr Peter Hiley; Mrs Anne Robbins; Beeston & District Local History Society; Nottinghamshire County Council; Nottinghamshire Archives Office; the staff at Beeston and Nottingham Libraries; the staff at Broxtowe Borough Council; The Ordnance Survey; The Public Records Office, Kew; The General Register Office; The British Newspaper Library.

Introduction

Early in the 19th century certain events occurred in Chilwell which were to put this insignificant village on the map. Events which, even to this day, are still sometimes talked about by residents of the area and which are known by most of the older inhabitants of the village - the story of the Ghost House and the Chilwell Ghost.

A number of 'myths' have been told about the Chilwell Ghost, such as that it was that of a woman who had been murdered by her husband who then cut off her head, or that a pedlar had murdered a family in a cottage, which was subsequently haunted by their restless spirits. These are just two of the tales that have been related to me. It is, of course, not surprising that after all these years the truth of what really happened has become exaggerated or twisted in the telling. However, many local people may know something of the true story; that it actually concerned a pedlar who went missing and was believed by many of the villagers to have been murdered by the inhabitants of a particularly lonely cottage, and that this cottage was then believed to be haunted by the ghost of the pedlar.

Another myth, which has found its way into at least one local history book, is that when the Inham Nook housing estate was being extended in the 1950s, the actual site of the Ghost House was deliberately not built over. In fact, as will be seen, this is not so and its actual location is now covered by other, newer houses.

From time to time, occasional references to the Chilwell Ghost have appeared in newspaper articles, and books of local interest have contained brief accounts of the story. However, to date, no serious attempt has ever been made at a detailed investigation into the true facts surrounding the story; to try and find contemporary accounts of the events and to identify the actual persons involved; to establish if and when a murder really did take place and whether this event had any connection with the subsequent reported haunting.

What follows is the result of my investigation into an intriguing episode in Chilwell's otherwise unremarkable history; a real life historical detective story and an attempt to solve an almost 200 year old mystery. I have long had an interest in matters of local history and was always, as a child, fascinated by the story of the Chilwell Ghost. I hope that those reading this book will derive as much pleasure from seeing the full story unfold as I did when researching it.

Finally, it is quite possible that this book might jog somebody's memory as to something related to them by grandparents or other older inhabitants of Chilwell on the subject of the Chilwell Ghost, or perhaps remind them of some other written accounts, documents or details which I have failed to discover. I would certainly be delighted to hear from anyone with further information.

CHAPTER ONE

THE CHILWELL GHOST STORY

Many of those reading this book may live in the Chilwell area and therefore be familiar with the locations referred to. However, in the hope that this story may have found its way further afield, and for anyone without local knowledge, it might be helpful to provide a brief description of the location of the events described in the following chapters.

Chilwell is situated about five miles west of Nottingham. Like many other former small agricultural villages near to large cities, much residential development has taken place over the past seventy years, and it is now primarily a largely residential area, situated between Beeston and Attenborough. The five mile journey from Chilwell to Nottingham is now entirely through built-up areas and there are no longer any farms in the village.

However, things were very much different in the 19th century when Chilwell was a small village, the inhabitants being mainly engaged in agriculture and framework knitting, a cottage industry very common in this part of Nottinghamshire. The village was a 'long' village, most of the houses stretching out along the High Road, or Turnpike Road as it then was, and surrounded by fields and orchards. Chilwell Hall, the ancestral home of the Charlton family, stood at the eastern end of the village, and there were three pubs, the *Charlton Arms*, the *Cadland* and the *Chequers* (all still in existence but much altered or rebuilt). For a short while in the early 1800s there was also the *Red Lion,* which still exists as a private residence.

To give an idea of its size, the population in 1801 was 638; in 1821, 823; in 1861, 910; in 1901, 1,176; in 1921, 2,125 and today it is about 12,000. It had no parish church until 1915, when Christ Church was consecrated; prior to that the parish church for Chilwell was at Attenborough, about a mile away. John Morris Wilson's *Imperial Gazetteer of England and Wales* of 1875 describes Chilwell as: 'A hamlet in Attenborough parish, Notts. near the River Trent and the Midland Railway 4½ miles SW of Nottingham. It has a post office under Nottingham. Real Property £5,003. Pop. 815. Houses 180. Stocking making is much carried on.'

Such was Chilwell, and no doubt for most of its inhabitants life continued year after year in the same old way, with little of excitement or interest to distract the population from the same old daily chores, until the late 1820s when an event occurred which was destined to become part of a local legend.

As mentioned in the introduction, many local people will have a vague idea of what the Chilwell Ghost story is all about. However, many others will not, and it is therefore necessary to set the scene by relating just what is supposed to have happened all those years ago.

There is probably no better way of doing this than to reproduce here the account given by Robert Mellors in his book *Attenborough Chilwell and Toton Then and Now*, published in 1919:

The Chilwell Ghost must be referred to, not as being one of the notables of the parish, for no one ever saw the ghost, yet the impression produced upon the public mind was so profound, the crowds of people that went to see and hear 'something' were so great, the mystery was so intricate, and remained unexplained, that some notice is required. The difficulty is that the stories told at the time were wild, and the printed accounts then published were incorrect, it is therefore necessary to fall back upon more sober judgement, and the following statement is according to the report repeatedly given by Mr J. R. Pearson to his sons, and to friends, and may be relied on, for Mr Pearson was a sensible, thoughtful, business man, and a large employer of labour in the parish.

The Ashflat house, commonly called the Ghost house, is a small cottage in the lane leading to Stapleford, at the foot of a hill covered by an orchard, both belonging to Mr Pearson, but the cottage had for a number of years been occupied by a workman, whom we will call 'X,' together with his family. About 1843 strange noises began to be heard at nights in this house, for something which sounded like a heavy mangold wurzel, or swede turnip, apparently was banged against the shutter with such force that it sometimes shook the glass out of the leaded window, but no trace of any missile could ever be found, nor of any marks on newly fallen snow, nor of footsteps, nor of anything having been dragged away. No amount of watching detected what caused the noise. Mr Pearson was determined to clear up the mystery, and he held the latch of the door below, ready to rush out, while his brother looked out of the window above. Quite a number of different plans for detection were formed, and carried out, without avail. One was that Mr Pearson had made, secretly, a frame the size of the window, with short legs at the four corners, in each of which was a spike. This he took up after dark, and driving out the visitors, of which the cottage was full, he removed the outside shutter, and placed the frame, which was covered with brown paper coated with lamp black and oil, in its place. At a yard or two distant it was impossible to tell this from the wooden shutter, but as the resisting power of brown paper soaked in oil is not great, they took care to stand clear of the window, and let whatever came have a clear course inside. They had not long to wait, for the blow came as usual, the window panes rattled, but nothing came inside, nor could a mark be found on the brown paper. Mr Pearson, being an amateur chemist, endeavoured to trace the matter to explosives, but every idea failed, and his reply to all questions as to what the thing was, always took the same form - 'I have given you the facts; you must draw your own conclusions'.

Such was the fame of the Chilwell Ghost that on Sundays the village resembled Goose Fair, special extra trains being run, and two publicans retired with fortunes. Doubtless many of the wild stories that were told emanated from their fertile brains, for, of course, the more dreadful the stories, the more people came, and the more liquor was consumed at the Charlton Arms and the Cadlands Inn.

At length the nuisance became so intolerable that the house was closed, and so remained for a long time. Afterwards an old cobbler who was badly off, begged that he might live there, and pay a small annual acknowledgement. It was pointed out to him that the house was lonely, being a long way from the village, but he persisted in his request, which was granted on the understanding that if anything more was heard about ghosts he would be turned out at once. His reply was that he had no fear of ghosts, and that 'the Lord would take care of him'. He lived in the house some twelve months, and then took back the key, and being questioned he said that ' while he did not believe in ghosts, it kept knocking, and knocking, till he got tired', in other words, it got upon his nerves. The house was thereupon closed, and has so remained ever since.

Here the historian must stop, and now comes the conjectural part of the story, for there was no police investigation. A certain pedlar, who did a considerable business amongst the cottagers, was missing. Many of them owed him money, and he never called for it. They made an inquiry as to who had seen him last and a man named 'S' who lived in a cottage attached to another orchard, said the pedlar called upon him some time in March, and on leaving asked permission to walk across his orchard, the lane being deep in mud, and saying that he was going to pass the night at the Ashflat house. Upon this a man 'L' who was for many years a parish constable, but who then lived at a house connected with another orchard on the Toton road, nearly a mile away, said that somewhere about that time he had a terrible dream, and was sure that something was wrong. He therefore got up and walked around his orchard, but found nothing and went back to bed, but he could not sleep, and after tossing about he got up again and walked right over the hill and down to the Ashflat orchard, and hearing sounds he walked quickly, and leaning over the gate he saw in the garden the occupier, 'X' and his son digging by the light of a lantern. He called out, and the men, who appeared very frightened, abused him for startling them at that hour of the morning, being about five o'clock. They said that as the wife had been up all night washing - she could be heard scrubbing in the house - they had got up early to make an onion bed, as the days were short. 'L' was satisfied with the explanation and returned home. One day during the apple harvest, when the workmen picnic out of doors, the man 'X' was dining with the rest, when his wife came for him, and after some altercation he threatened to kick her if she did not go home. She replied 'You dare not. I could hang you any day. I have your coat of arms in the bedroom!' When 'X' was gone the others asked each other the meaning of the words the woman had spoken, and they came to the conclusion that they had reference to the pedlar.

Amongst other things it was stated that the daughter of 'X' gave away to friends print stuff which she said her aunt had given to her, but no one knew of her aunt, and they wondered how people could afford to be so generous. Eventually the family removed. Mrs 'X' died, and in her last illness either 'X' or his son was always with her, and it was said that she was not allowed to see either doctor or parson alone. After a lapse of time 'X' being left by his family, married again. His second wife was said to have had a very uneasy time, and when he was on his death-bed she fled to the nearest cottage, some quarter of a mile distant, and said she could stay with him no longer; that night after night he sat up in bed, and pointing to the corner of the room cried out 'There he is! I murdered him, and buried the axe in the brook'. The neighbour returned with the terrified wife, and found the man dead. The axe was found years afterwards in the brook by a man named 'S' who showed it to persons now living (1919), but the body of the pedlar was never found. Such were the common reports and belief. No police investigations were ever made, and therefore rumours remained untested, and the people who were acquainted with the circumstances settled down to the belief that the noises were made by a disembodied spirit endeavouring to call attention to a crime.

The above constitutes the generally accepted version of events. A similar, shortened version appeared in the March 1973 newsletter of the Beeston & District Local History Society, where the following item was included, having been submitted by Mr A. L. Searle of Cator Lane, Chilwell, a then member of the society:

Referring to the Chilwell Ghost House Story, this was well known to all the young children of the village, and there is no doubt that many of the older and less knowledgeable people really believed the house was haunted. My mother often reported the following story relating to it, and it seemed to have been told to her by her parents: 'At one time the ghost house was inhabited by a somewhat doubtful family, a man and wife and daughter. The house of course was in a secluded part of the district and the old lane led out towards Toton across the fields. At this time there was a pedlar who visited the district carrying his bag of cloth, silk and ribbon lengths, and he was well known in the district. On a fine day he told the local people that he was going out to the Chilwell area, and he was known to have set off in that direction. Strangely, he was never seen again in the district. Some months after his disappearance the daughter of the ghost house dwellers appeared dressed in some cloths and ribbons that the pedlar was known to be carrying at the time he set out in that direction. Dark hints, making suggestions of dark deeds, were rife in the area, but there never seemed to be any solution to the mystery of the pedlar who disappeared.' The suggestion of a ghost creating the mysterious knockings was always associated with the story. However, my grandfather often told that he was actually present when bones were unearthed in the orchard surrounding the old house.

That the story was so widely known in the area at the time can be judged by the fact that it earned such a long account in Robert Mellor's book. Furthermore, it was also mentioned by Leonard Jacks in his book *The Great Houses of Nottinghamshire and the County Families*, published in 1881. In his chapter about Chilwell Hall, he says:

The house at Chilwell, which for so long a period has been owned by the Charltons, forms part of a village whose rusticity has not yet been destroyed by such building operations as those which have gone on in the heart and outskirts of its neighbour Beeston, once extensively owned by the Charlton family. It has retained its village aspect and its village life, and some of its inhabitants have a distinct belief, that a house standing out in the fields is inhabited by a ghost, which however, never found its way into their last census papers, and is, therefore, not accounted for. This is the restless spirit of a man who was mysteriously murdered in the locality within the memory of many living, and whose body was never discovered. Persons who have tenanted this house in the fields, have spoken of noises in the night and phantom-play of that kind, but none has ever seen anything approaching the popular notion of what a ghost is like, so that the people who hear about the spectre are reasonably sceptical. Between the Chilwell ghost and Chilwell Hall there is nothing in common, except perhaps something which comes of the fact that the principal family in the village is kept au courant concerning the proceedings of the spirit who might perhaps find that appropriate calm, which would confine him to his own resources when he felt the need of diversion, that now assumes the form of pranks with shutters or windows, if he could be induced to take up his abode in the dark and ancient cellars of the hall.

Such is the story of the Chilwell Ghost. It has been handed down from parents to children over the years, and no doubt some of the details will have become confused or changed in the telling. However, the events as told are usually similar to the above versions. There are a few variations in the detail between these accounts; Mellor's version states that the pedlar went to the Ash Flat House in March, when the lane was 'deep in mud'. Mr Searle's mother's version states it was 'on a fine day' when the pedlar told people he was setting off for Chilwell, but such minor differences can be accepted as part of the difficulty in relying on oral tradition. However, as we shall discover later, newspaper reports stated that the murder took place 'towards the close of the year just named'.

Following the publication of Mellors' book in 1919, there was a renewed interest in the subject of the Chilwell Ghost, and some correspondence appeared in local newspapers. However, no further new evidence or facts emerged. Robert Mellors stated that his account was based on the report repeatedly given by Mr J. R. Pearson to his sons and friends, and in his book he acknowledged the contribution of Mr A. H. Pearson in regard to details of the Chilwell Ghost. Alfred Hetley Pearson was a son of John Royston Pearson, who had died in 1876. It should also be remembered that the actual events had occurred over ninety years before Mellors' book was published. There is no evidence that Mellors consulted any contemporary documents, and in one important respect he is in error. He stated that it was in 1843 that the occupants of the Ash Flat House went to Mr Pearson, their landlord, to report the strange happenings. But as we shall see later, the haunting actually started during the winter of 1837/38. This demonstrates how facts and details can become confused over the years, and we should also allow for the exaggeration which must surely have taken place as tales were handed from parent to child.

For example, the story of the former parish constable, who, after having a strange dream walked to the Ash Flat House and found the occupant and his son digging in the garden, whilst his wife was inside scrubbing, might have some basis in fact. But the clear implication in this account is that father and son were burying the body of the pedlar whilst the wife was inside, busy cleaning up the bloodstains! It makes a good story but exactly how true is it?

Mellors also states that special trains were organised to bring people to the area to view the Ghost House. This might be true, although no documentary evidence has been found to substantiate this claim. The initial excitement over the haunting started during the winter of 1837/38, but the Midland Counties Railway between Nottingham and Derby did not open until 4th June 1839, some eighteen months after the first reports of the haunting. There was a station at Beeston from the opening of the line, but Attenborough Station, the nearest station to Chilwell, did not open until December 1856.

Special trains are known to have been organised from both Nottingham and Derby to Beeston for the annual wakes week in July 1839, and it is possible that some of the passengers on these trains also took the opportunity to view the Ghost House. This seems the most likely explanation, as the story of the Ghost House is supposed to have become famous for many miles around, and it is quite likely that it was still of sufficient interest to have been fresh in the public mind throughout 1839.

CHAPTER TWO

THE GHOST HOUSE

The 'Ashflat' is an old name for the area of land under discussion. An early reference to it can be found in Alfred Edward Lawson Lowe's *History of the Hundred of Broxtowe, Part II* (published privately c.1870). Under a section on Charitable Benefactors he refers to the will of Thomas Charlton of Chilwell Esq., dated 12th March 1689, in which '. . . he devised to Thomas Charlton Esq., his son and heir, and to his heirs a close called "Ashflat" . . . . . . charged with the yearly payments of £4 .6. 0 to the poor of Chilwell and Attenborough . . .'

At some later date ownership of the Ashflat passed to the Pearson family, of whom Lawson Lowe said '. . . an estate of some extent is owned by Mr John Royston Pearson, a noted horticulturalist, whose nursery gardens at Chilwell have a well-merited reputation.' The Pearson family owned it until 1892 when they sold much of their land in Chilwell by auction (see Chapter 7).

However, from the late 1830s onwards it was always referred to as the 'Ghost House' and the lane which led to it became known as 'Ghost House Lane'. The house itself was demolished about 1952/53 as the new Inham Nook housing estate was gradually being extended, but until the mid-1960s, Ghost House Lane itself remained as a narrow country lane leading off Field Lane, which was itself a country lane bounded on each side by fields. Halfway along Field Lane on the right-hand side, another building is marked on both maps. This was the former Keeper's Cottage belonging to the Chilwell Hall Estate. The whole area is now residential, but Ghost House Lane remains as a footpath off Field Lane.

The maps included here show the area at various dates over a period of almost two centuries. The earliest known large scale map is the Chilwell Estate Map of 1829 and an extract from this is shown overleaf. Road names have been inserted here to enable a comparison to be made with later maps.

The Ordnance Survey 25 inch to the mile map of 1901 marks the Ghost House, although Ghost House Lane itself is not named. Indeed, until the area became built up in the 1960s the lane was never provided with a name, although more recent maps do name it thus. It will be noticed that the house shown on the 1901 map is in an identical position to the building shown on the 1829 map. Exactly when it was built is not known, but from old photographs it would appear to date from about the late 18th or early 19th century. It stood in a small valley, through which ran a brook, running south on a meandering course and eventually reaching the River Trent. In recent years most of this brook has been culverted, although it still remains as an open brook a short distance away from the site of the Ghost House.

The **exact** location where the house stood is difficult to determine by observation alone, such has been the scale of development in the area. However, by a detailed comparison of old and new maps, of council plans dating from 1952, and from measurements taken at the location, it is clear that it stood on the site now occupied by the two houses at the corner of Valley Road and Pearson Avenue (see photograph on page 31).

An extract from the Chilwell Estate Map dated 1829. A comparison with the 1901 O.S. map opposite shows just how little had altered. Note the Ash Flat House in the identical position shown on the O.S. map. (Courtesy of Mr Roy Davies)

An extract from the 1901 O.S. 25 inch to the mile map (scale reduced).

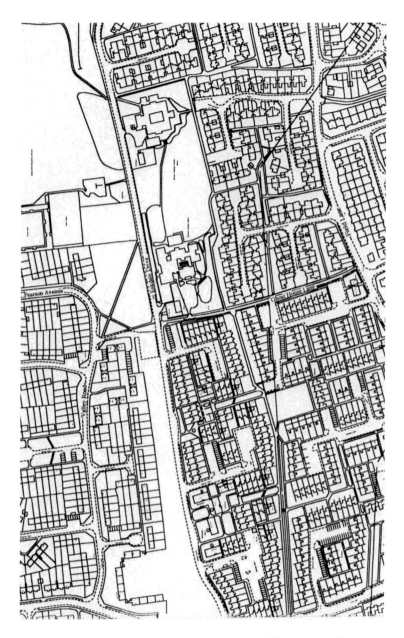

An extract from a recent O.S. 25 inch to the mile map (scale reduced).
The Ghost House stood at the corner of Valley Road and Pearson Avenue.
(Reproduced from the Ordnance Survey map with the permission of the Controller of
Her Majesty's Stationery Office. © Crown Copyright MC 8671M0001)

CHAPTER THREE

THE GHOST STORY IN RHYME

From time to time accounts of the Chilwell Ghost appeared in the press. The *Nottingham Weekly Guardian* for many years carried a column entitled 'Local Notes and Queries' which consisted of items of historical interest. Its edition of 27th May 1927 contained extracts from Robert Mellor's account, as shown in Chapter 1. The same edition also printed a most interesting 'Rhymed Account' of the events at Chilwell all those years ago. The item reads as follows:

RHYMED ACCOUNT OF CHILWELL GHOST

In reply to our correspondent's inquiry for information respecting the Chilwell Ghost, Mr Harry Packer, Beeston, kindly forwards the following rhymed account of the mysterious circumstances supposed to be associated with the Ghost House, from a long set of verses entitled 'The Chilwell Ghost' published locally about seventy years ago. In spite of obvious little faults the ballad is a literary achievement picturing up the scenes with vivid simplicity akin to the grim horror of the 'Dream of Eugene Aram'.

Author's note: Eugene Aram (1704 - 1759). Born in the West Riding, he was a schoolmaster at Knaresborough and in 1754 was tried and acquitted on a charge of being concerned in the disappearance of a local shoemaker. After achieving some distinction as a philologist, he was arrested at Lynn in Norfolk following the discovery of a skeleton in a cave at Knaresborough. He was tried at York, confessed to the murder after his conviction and was hanged. He is the subject of a poem, 'The Dream of Eugene Aram' by Thomas Hood. This murder case bears some similarities to the Chilwell story.

Broadside ballads of this nature were very popular in the 19th century, and events of a sensational nature such as famous trials, public executions, or the more scandalous political or royal events were quickly seized upon by local publishers as a source of quick profit, and a poem would soon be written, printed and rushed out for sale on the streets. It is not known exactly when this poem first appeared, nor who wrote it.

The *Weekly Guardian's* item of 27th May stated that the poem was 'published locally about seventy years ago' which would date it to about 1857. However, for reasons that will become apparent, I suspect that it probably first appeared in 1850. Nevertheless, what follows is certainly a fascinating piece of social history and is one more example of the widespread interest that was generated in the area by the disappearance of a pedlar, his alleged murder and the subsequent reported haunting of the house where the foul deed was believed to have been committed.

The Chilwell Ghost

Many the scenes portrayed in rhyme,
Many a tale of olden time,
Many a deed of foulest crime;
Many a plot, many a fight,
Many a ghost arrayed in white,
Many a murder done at night!
Oft has the bard, with wondrous skill,
Called forth his powers of mind and will,
And with his paper and his quill
Presented to the public eye,
In colours of the deepest dye,
These deeds of blood and mystery -
But I will add in simple strain,
Another to the awful train.
Down against an orchard,
A red-bricked cottage stands,
Whose fame has spread o'er this,
And spread o'er other lands.
Behind it fruit trees grow,
Before it ran a brook,
On either hand broad fields -
A pleasant lovely nook.
That homestead, pretty and neat,
Was a quiet, lonely spot,
Inhabitants and house
Apparently forgot.
The day then slowly advanced,
And slowly departed the night,
With little fresh or new
From morning's dawn to evening's flight.
Amongst the scanty travellers
Who chanced to pass this way,
Amongst the scanty visitors
Who ope'd this lonely door
And said to its dwellers 'Good day'
Was a packman.
No matter the weather to him;
If rainy or dry, or scorching or cold,
His goods must be hawked, His things must be sold;
He never must keep at home for a day,
But up he must be at his work far away . . .

From year to year, along this lonely road,
Was seen this packman with his heavy load,
But always gladly he approached this home
And pleased the inmates were to see him come.
His bundles soon were carefully untied,
And every ware and trinket keenly eyed;
But well for him if he had passed them by,
And to that building never turned his eye,
Nor ever stood upon its red-bricked floor,
Nor ever raised his hand to ope its door.
Poor packman - thine a solemn, awful end!
The love for thee from those within was feigned;
Their tongues could flatter, and their lips could smile
But they could plan a bloody murder while! . . .

The Plot to Kill the Pedlar

That night he filled their homely chair,
And there he ate his evening fare;
That night he had a friendly chat
With those within, who round him sat.
Out-tired with his toilsome walk,
And weary of the evening's talk,
Dull, drowsy, with the heated blaze
Which shone upon his honest face,
His heavy eyelids drooped and closed,
And soon in sleep he there reposed.
'We cannot have a better time
To perpetrate, unseen the crime;
Come, let us kill, and take his gold
And thus grow rich ere we grow old.'
Thus, thus, these hard ones thought and spake,
And did for filthy lucre's sake.
For, while the sleeper soundly slept,
The master gently, slowly, crept
Into the little room behind,
The deadly instrument to find.
He brought a hatchet hanging there,
And came and stood behind the chair;
Then raised his arm, and took good aim,
And swiftly, down the weapon came.
'Neath such a sure and signal stroke
The pedlar from his sleep awoke,

But not as from a pleasant dream.
He woke but could not call or scream;
He woke to take his last, short, breath,
Then died - a sudden awful death.
But now the blood must disappear,
From off the floor, seat, everywhere;
The body must be put away -
And all before the break of day.
With noiseless steps they ope'd the door,
To hearken and to watch before
They ventured out, to dig with spade
The grave where he must now be laid.
As nought was seen, and nothing heard,
They went and cautiously interred
Beneath a tree, at evening's noon,
By light which glimmered from the moon,
The murdered, all but headless, form
Of him who never meant them harm.
They roughly forced his body in,
And tried - as though no spade had been -
To cover up with weeds and grass,
That those who there might chance to pass,
Could see no change about the spot
Where soon they hoped his bones would rot.
Quick, stealthily, they hastened back,
To clean the bricks and hide his pack,
This done, to bed - but not to sleep;
No slumber o'er those eyes would creep;
That night a week to them appeared,
They thought, they trembled, and they feared,
But could not sleep; again they saw
The bloody scene, which filled with awe
Their heated minds; again, again,
It rose before their eyes. In vain
They strove to think of aught besides;
In vain they strove the scene to hide;
There was the hatchet lifted high -
The fall - his faint yet dying cry -
Blood coming from his severed veins -
His garments covered with its stains -
His struggles, twitching, agonies -
His last short gasp, and glazing eyes!

The Haunted House

Time rolled along, and soon drew near,
The day when packman should appear;
But no one saw him in the lane,
Or in the fields, on hill or plain;
None heard the tramping of his feet,
His well known whistle in the street.
Thinking, perchance he might be ill,
The public waited on until
Another of his days came round,
To see if he might then be found.
It came, but not with tidings fraught,
Respecting him: in vain they sought,
Listened and looked around in vain;
They never saw his face again.
A cry, a general cry was made,
But none could render any aid;
Who saw him last they knew full well,
And more than that but few could tell;
They would not, could not, dare not say -
So it remained a mystery.
He - dark assassin - quitted soon
The house in which the deed was done,
He left it empty, lonely, bare,
And sought another homestead, where
Fresh scenes might banish far away
The thoughts that probed him night and day.
But doubtless there he could not rest,
Those thoughts, like spectres still oppressed.
Suspicion, like a monster, seized
The public mind, still unappeased;
And lifting up the doubtful veil,
Pointed to him that fills my tale -
But justice followed up too slow.
And let the guilty murderer go.
But this all knew - they who before
Were plain, and miserably poor,
At once grew rich, and well supplied;
And likewise this, each of them died
A dark, an awful, horrid death,
As if to show the Almighty's wrath.

The house was occupied again,
By some hard working - honest man.
He and his wife soon plainly heard,
When they were certain no one stirred,
A noise so singular and queer,
It shook and startled them with fear.
Early next day their neighbours knew;
Who, wondering if it could be true,
Half doubted, half believed. Once more,
A sound as loud as that before
Went ringing through the darkened air.
This time a neighbour sitting there,
Who fairly heard as well as they
The noise which filled them with dismay -
The thing was clearly understood
To be a fact. The multitude
Believed, and spread it far and wide,
Scores, hundreds, came within that year,
These strange, these nightly sounds to hear;
To get a glimpse of ghost in white,
They watched and watched for many a night,
Some said they saw him, headless, stalk
Along the narrow garden walk,
Then, in a moment, disappear.
Some heard a rustling on the stair;
Raps on the shutter in the dark,
Yet leaving not the slightest mark.
'Twere well if some had kept at home,
And left this house and ghost alone;
So preyed its stories on their mind
Their reason fled, and left behind
What once was deemed a casket fair,
To lie deserted, waste and bare,
Naught, naught could bring it back again;
Wild they became, and wild they kept,
Till in the sleep of death they slept.
And now my simple verse is done,
Bring prejudice, contempt, or fun,
The main is true. The man was missed -
The things were seen - the sounds were list -
The ghost house can be viewed today,
And scores affirm what now I say.

CHAPTER FOUR

WHO KILLED THE PEDLAR?

For many years I have collected any anecdotes or references I have come across relating to the Chilwell Ghost. One of the most significant references I had found some years ago was an item which appeared in the *Nottinghamshire Guardian* in 1888. The item reads as follows:

THURSDAY Feb. 16th. On this day, in 1850, John Baguley died at Chilwell, near Nottingham, making confession in his last moments of having murdered a hawker, whose body he disposed of, and whose property he stole and sold. Baguley was seventy years old at his demise, and the murder was committed about a quarter of a century before. The most extraordinary feature of the case arose out of the circumstances that the cottage in which the deed was performed was said to be so persistently haunted by a ghost that as to be virtually untenantable. People when they took it declared that they could not stay, and the 'Chilwell Ghost' was the cause of anxiety and dread to thousands all around the district. Adventurous sceptics entered into possession of the premises without number, and visitors inspected the tenement from many places in the area extending to more than a hundred miles around. They all declared that noises were to be heard, that cups and saucers rattled, and whether empty, or full, the cottage was never free from groans, taps, and other mysterious sounds. The occupant of it disappeared very suddenly, but, as he was a hawker, no suspicion arose respecting the cause. At one time he had been a sweetheart of Baguley's daughter, and her father denounced him as a recreant lover, in which his neighbours agreed. On the death of his first wife Baguley married again, and disturbed his spouse by a strange conduct. He would jump up in bed and make exclamations of an extraordinary kind, and on the day before he died he cried out whilst asleep, 'the pick I did it with is in the dyke.' Next morning, being told he had only a very short time to live, he confessed to the murder and robbery. Subsequently a bundle of clothes, stained with blood, was found in an attic, and a pick was fished out of an adjacent dyke. The popular tradition is that the noises ceased when Baguley died, and the haunted cottage at Chilwell found a permanent tenant. This was only thirty-eight years ago.

This report raises a number of interesting points. It implies that the Ghost House was inhabited by the **pedlar**, whereas all the other accounts state that the Ghost House was where the **murderer** lived. As we shall soon discover, the Ash Flat House was, indeed, the home of the supposed murderer.

This just shows that journalistic licence and unreliable newspaper accounts are nothing new. Also, it seemed likely that this account, appearing thirty-eight years after the death of John Baguley, must have relied on earlier accounts printed at the time of his death; as will be seen later, this turned out to be the case.

Despite any factual errors, for the paper actually to name the person allegedly responsible for a murder would imply an element of truth. I therefore determined to try and find out as much as possible about this John Baguley and draw up a family tree for him. When was he born? Who were his parents? When and whom did he marry? Did he have any children? For we now had a name for the alleged murderer!

Anyone who has ever spent time tracing their ancestors will know of the sources of information available when trying to confirm the dates for a person's birth, baptism, marriage and death. The principal sources are parish registers and the civil registration of births, marriages and deaths. The compulsory keeping of parish registers commenced in 1538, and although some early registers are no longer in existence for various reasons, the majority of 19th century ones are. Civil registration started in 1837, and whilst it did not become legally compulsory until 1857 there is usually a good chance of being able to trace the event. A copy of any certificate can be obtained on payment of a small fee.

The first step was to try and confirm whether a man named John Baguley had died at Chilwell on 16th February 1850. As stated in the introduction, Chilwell did not yet have its own parish church, Attenborough then being the parish church for Chilwell, so that the inhabitants of Chilwell would most likely be baptised, married and buried at Attenborough Church.

The Nottinghamshire Archives Office has microfiche copies of all surviving Nottinghamshire parish registers. I began a search of these and in the Attenborough parish register found the following entry:

Buried, 12 February 1850. John Baguley of Attenborough, aged 61

This seemed to be confirmation of the newspaper account, despite a few minor discrepancies which can easily be accounted for. The newspaper gave the date of death as 16th February, whilst the burial actually took place on 12th February. The death would have occurred a few days earlier, and this was to be verified when a copy of his death certificate was obtained. The age of John Baguley also varies - the newspaper said 'about 70' whilst the parish register said 61. However, in the 19th century and earlier there are often discrepancies between various documents in relation to a person's age, particularly where older people are concerned. As civil registration did not commence until 1837, some people did not know exactly how old they were, and the age entered in the parish register by the churchwarden would be based on information given by relatives or friends - and this information might have been wrong. Also, the newspaper account may have relied on information given by someone who may not have known his exact age.

It seems likely, however, that this John Baguley was about 61, as a subsequent search in the Attenborough parish register revealed the following entry:

Baptised 29 June 1788. John, son of Joseph and Mary Bagguley

Apart from the spelling of the surname with a double 'g', this appeared to be the same John Baguley who died 61 years later. Spelling was often somewhat haphazard at that time, and names are often found with slight variations in the spelling. The next step was to obtain a copy of his death certificate, as this might contain further information not shown in the parish register. A copy of this is reproduced overleaf. The death certificate confirms that his age was indeed 61, as shown in the parish register, and that he died of 'paralysis' on 8th February 1850. Unfortunately, his exact address is not given, only 'Chilwell - Attenboro'. The informant of his death was Joseph Baguley, whom we will soon discover was his eldest son.

Having now established John Baguley's actual date of death and his age, the next step was to do a much more detailed search to try and find as many details as possible about his parents, his marriage and the baptism of any children. Since he had been born about 1788, I tried to find a record of his marriage. In those days, men tended to marry at about the age of 21, often after having completed an apprenticeship, although marriage at an earlier age was not uncommon.

Despite an extensive search, I was unable to find any marriage involving a John Baguley at Attenborough or other local churches. Of course, it was not certain that he had married in Attenborough. Just as today, marriages tended to take place at the bride's church, and if his wife came from elsewhere the marriage could have taken place at another church. Fortunately, a number of marriage indexes exist, covering most parishes in the country, so it was relatively easy to see whether there was any record of a John Baguley having married.

The indexes for Nottinghamshire showed only one such entry, a marriage that took place on 17th December 1805 between John Baguley and Jane Maddock at Ratcliffe-on-Soar, a small village south of the River Trent, about five miles from Attenborough. I thought this date might be a little too early, as John would only have been about 17 at the time. However, I looked up the entry, which shows that John Baguley was from Attenborough. A copy of the entry in the parish register is shown on page 22. This proves that he had married at a very early age. I checked to see if I

CERTIFIED COPY of an ENTRY OF DEATH
Pursuant to the Births and Deaths Registration Act 1953

Registration District Shardlow

1850. Death in the Sub-district of Stapleford in the County of Nottingham & Derby

No.	When and where died	Name and surname	Sex	Age	Occupation	Cause of death	Signature, description, and residence of informant	When registered	Signature of registrar
30	Eighth February 1850 Chilwell Attenboro'	John Baguley	Male	61 Years	Labourer	Paralysis 1 month Certified	X The mark of Joseph Baguley Present at the Death Chilwell Attenboro'	Eleventh February 1850	J W Cade Registrar.

Certified to be a true copy of an entry in a register in my custody.

A copy of John Baguley's death certificate.
(Courtesy of the General Register Office)

could find anything about his wife. A Jane Maddock had been baptised at Ratcliffe-on-Soar on 24th November 1784, the daughter of John Maddock and his wife Ann. This is almost certainly the same Jane Maddock, as when she died in November 1841 both the burial entry in the Attenborough parish register and her death certificate give her age as 58.

Having found when and where John and Jane were married, I then made a search in the Attenborough parish registers to see whether there were any entries for the baptism of children named Baguley, with parents named John and Jane. The following entries were found:

Attenborough Parish Church, register of baptisms

6 Mar. 1814	*Maria, dau of John and Jane Baguley of Attenborough, FWK*
1 Sept. 1816	*Joseph, son of John and Jane Baguley of Attenborough, FWK*
30 May 1819	*Jane, dau of John and Jane Baguley of Attenborough, FWK*
18 Sept.1821	*Benjamin, son of John and Jane Baguley of Chilwell, labourer*
20 Feb. 1832	*Edward Thomas, base son of Diana Baguley of Chilwell, servant*
27 Jan. 1835	*Louis, base son of Diana Baguley of Chilwell, servant*
25 Dec. 1836	*Emma, base dau. of Diana Baguley of Chilwell, stocking maker*

---

n.b. 'base' is an archaic word for illegitimate, often used in parish registers.

These entries showed that John and Jane Baguley had four children baptised at Attenborough, and it also indicated that John's occupation was originally a FWK (framework knitter), but by the time Benjamin was baptised in 1821 he was a labourer.

The last three baptisms listed, all illegitimate children of Diana Baguley have been included here, because although they were not children of John and Jane Baguley, they were later to prove a significant part of the story.

Census returns are another invaluable source of information, and I looked to see if I could find John Baguley and his family in the 1841 Census, carried out on 6th June that year. A detailed census has been taken in this country every ten years from 1841 and copies of each county's census returns can usually be found on microfilm or microfiche in libraries or record offices. Fortunately, indexes exist by surname of all the entries in the census returns, so all that is required is to check the indexes for a particular name, and then consult the appropriate reference to find the details of those persons.

The 1841 Census (unlike all later ones) did not show the exact relationship between the persons living in the same household, nor was the actual place of birth shown, only whether the person was born in that county. So far as age is concerned, the actual age was only shown for children aged under 15; thereafter ages were shown in 5 year bands, i.e. aged 15 to 19 shown as 15, aged 20 to 24 shown as 20 and so on. As with parish registers, one should be wary of putting too much trust in ages shown in census returns, as many people, particularly the elderly, often did not know exactly how old they were. Also, the information written down by the enumerator was what he was told, and the person giving the information might have been unsure about the exact ages of other members of the household.

The entry in the Ratcliffe-on-Soar parish register, showing the marriage of John Baguley and Jane Maddock. 17th December 1805. (Courtesy Nottinghamshire Archives Office)

Nevertheless, despite these shortcomings, census returns remain an invaluable source of material in tracing one's ancestors. I checked all the entries for persons named Baguley living in the Chilwell and Attenborough areas. The name is not uncommon in Nottinghamshire, and there were two families of that name in the Chilwell area. It was fairly easy to eliminate the irrelevant family and the correct entry was found on Folio 19. A copy of the relevant part of Folio 19 is shown overleaf. The Ash Flat House was to the north of the Turnpike Road (the main road through the village), and the census therefore proves that by this date the Baguleys were not living in the Ash Flat House. As we shall see, this fact was also confirmed from other sources.

Each folio is in two pages. John Baguley appears at the bottom of the first page, the rest of his family on the next page. Note also Lewis Baguley living two doors away. 'Ag. lab.' is short for agricultural labourer. Actual addresses were generally not shown in the 1841 Census, at least in rural areas, where streets were often not named and houses were not numbered. Chilwell South Side was defined as '*All that part of the Parish of Chilwell South of the Nottingham & Birmingham Turnpike road, as far as the Brook including also the Boat House over the Trent.*'

We know from the Attenborough parish registers that John and Jane had at least four children, but the 1841 Census only shows Benjamin, plus a nine-year-old boy named Edward. Who was this Edward and where were the other children? The census only lists the persons actually present in the household on the day the census was taken and some of the children might have been elsewhere. Of course, some might have died young, a not unusual occurrence in the 19th century. I therefore checked the various parish registers for the burial of persons named Baguley and the following relevant entries were found:

Attenborough Parish Church, register of burials

14 June	*1812*	*Maria, infant dau. of John and Jane Baguley*
1 October	*1834*	*Maria Baguley of Chilwell, aged 20*
24 February	*1839*	*Emma Baguley of Chilwell, aged 2 years*
23 May	*1841*	*Diana Baguley of Chilwell, aged 29*
24 November	*1841*	*Jane Baguley of Chilwell, aged 58*
28 August	*1842*	*Jane Baguley of Chilwell, aged 23*
12 February	*1850*	*John Baguley of Attenborough, aged 61*

This showed that John and Jane's daughter Maria had died in 1834, whilst her sister Jane had died in 1842. Jane's whereabouts on 6th June 1841 when the census was taken is not known, but she could have been working away, perhaps in service. Joseph, however, was found living with a Samuel Capestick and his wife:

23

1841 Census. HO 107 / 855 Folio 19 Chilwell South Side.

(Crown copyright material in the Public Records Office. Reproduced by permission of the Controller of Her Majesty's Stationery Office)

1841 Census. HO 107 / 855		Folio 23	Chilwell South Side.
Name	*Age*	*Occupation*	*Born in this county*
Samuel Capestick	60	FWK	Yes
Elizabeth Capestick	60		Yes
Joseph Baguley	20	Ag. lab.	Yes

But to return to the nine-year-old Edward Baguley who appeared in the 1841 Census. He was unlikely to have been another child of John and Jane, as Jane would have been about 49 when she gave birth, but he was presumably a relative. He was, in fact, their grandson. His mother was the Diana who gave birth to three illegitimate children, of whom Edward Thomas was the first, baptised on 20th February 1832. The Emma Baguley who had died aged 2 in 1839 was the second of Diana Baguley's illegitimate children. Her third illegitimate child, Louis (or Lewis) was found in the 1841 Census living two doors away from John and Jane Baguley - see the extract opposite.

Diana was, therefore, another daughter of John and Jane, but her baptism does not appear in the Attenborough or other local parish registers. And who was the *Maria, infant dau. of John and Jane Baguley,* who was buried on 14th June 1812?

The answer to this puzzle was solved by consulting a number of baptism indexes that exist, and eventually I found the following extract in the parish registers for St. Leodegarius Church at Basford (now a suburb of Nottingham, but then a village, about six miles from Chilwell).

14 July 1811 Diana and Maria, daughters of John and Jane Baguley baptised.

So it seems that at some time after their marriage in 1805, John and Jane moved to Basford, and whilst living there they had two daughters, both baptised on the same day and, most likely, twins. It is possible that they might have moved to Basford to find work and also because that is where John's brother Joseph was living. He had been born about 1785 (baptised Attenborough 13th March 1785). No further records of Joseph are to be found in the Attenborough and Chilwell areas, but a Joseph Baguley married a Mary Gwynn at Basford St. Leodegarius Church on 23rd June 1806, and this might possibly be John's brother.

Shortly after Diana and Maria were baptised, the family must have moved back to Chilwell, where one of the girls, Maria, died in infancy. They subsequently named their next daughter Maria but she only lived to reach 20 and was buried on 1st

October 1834. The unfortunate Diana died of consumption aged just 29, on 21st May 1841, leaving two young children. She was buried at Attenborough two days later. It was not uncommon in the 19th century for young children to be left as orphans and they are often to be found in census returns living with in-laws or neighbours, as in this case; Edward with his grandparents and Lewis with neighbours Obed and Ann Osmond.

We have now built up a clear picture of John Baguley, his wife and children but I was also keen to find some details of his parents and grandparents. His father was Joseph Baguley, born about 1740, himself the son of Joseph Baguley and Frances Hardey, who were married at Attenborough on 7th June 1739. John's father Joseph married twice. His first wife was Mary Ballard, whom he married at Attenborough on 29th December 1772. No children have been found from this marriage and Mary died five years later in 1777. Joseph then married Mary Aram at Attenborough on 22nd April 1783, and they had three children, Joseph (1785), John (1788) and Frances (1790). John's father Joseph died in November 1793 and was buried at Attenborough on 15th of that month. One year later, his widow Mary married Henry Day.

Fortunately, Joseph left a will, and a copy of this is shown as Appendix A. He was described as a victualler and was almost certainly the landlord of the *Bell Inn*. This pub (now called the *Bluebell*) still exists at Attenborough, situated on the main road from Nottingham to Long Eaton, having been built there in the 1930s. However, the original *Bell Inn* stood in the village of Attenborough and is now a private house. The will shows that Joseph left his three children £20 each. Henry Day, who subsequently married Joseph's widow Mary is also mentioned in the will as a 'good friend'.

It would appear that, having married the widow Mary Baguley, Henry then became the victualler at the *Bell Inn*. The 1844 edition of Whites Commercial Directory for Nottinghamshire states that Henry Day was victualler at the *Blue Bell* in Attenborough, and was also the Parish Clerk. By 1853 his son Edward Day (John Baguley's half-brother) had taken over from his father both as victualler and Parish Clerk. The Days are a very old Attenborough family and the office of Parish Clerk at Attenborough has been held by the family for about three hundred years, only coming to an end in 1992.

The names of Ballard, Aram and Day are common names in Chilwell and Attenborough, and the Attenborough parish registers contain many references to persons of these names. The name Ballard will appear later in this story, as will the name Lee, one of the witnesses to Joseph Baguley's will.

The years 1841 and 1842 were not good for John Baguley. His daughter Diana died in May 1841 and then on 22nd November his wife Jane died of 'disease of the lungs'.

The following August his only surviving daughter Jane also died, aged 23. According to various accounts, when John Baguley died he was living with his second wife, so I searched for a record of his second marriage. No record of this marriage could be found at any of the local churches, but by searching the national indexes of the registration of marriages, I eventually found a John Baguley who had married in 1847 in the registration district of Shardlow (which included the Chilwell and Attenborough areas), and the details on the marriage certificate, reproduced below, prove this to be our man. On 9th September 1847, he had married Mary Smith of Barton, a widow, born Mary Woolley. The marriage had taken place in the register office at Shardlow, and one of the witnesses was Henry Day, possibly John's stepfather, or more likely a half-brother.

(Reproduced courtesy of the General Register Office)

So this was the woman who, as will be seen in the next chapter, was so alarmed by John's behaviour during his dying days, and who fled in fright from their cottage. I tried to find her in the 1851 Census, since if she was still alive she should have appeared as a 'Mrs Baguley, widow'. No such person could be found in the Chilwell or Attenborough areas. Perhaps after the shock of her husband's death-bed confession to murder she had moved away. However, John's two sons were to be found living in Chilwell as is shown in the following extract from the census return:

1851 Census HO 107 / 2141 Folio 102 Chilwell, south of Turnpike Road

Name	Status	Age	Occupation	Born
Joseph Baguley	Head	32 UM	Ag. lab.	Notts. Attenboro'
Benjamin Baguley	Bro'	28 UM	Ag. lab.	Notts. Chilwell
Thomas Baguley	Stepson	19 UM	Bricklayers lab.	Notts. Chilwell

---

Joseph was the head of the family and living with him were his brother Benjamin and his 'stepson' Thomas Baguley, all three unmarried (UM in the census). Since Joseph was unmarried, Thomas could clearly not be a stepson as we now understand the term. Thomas is clearly Edward Thomas, the illegitimate son of Joseph's deceased sister Diana, and therefore his nephew. The use of certain terms to define relationships has changed somewhat since the 19th century, and words such as 'stepson' and 'in-law' were often used haphazardly to define relationships of an irregular nature, including illegitimate relatives.

Such are the details of the Baguley family. I have made no attempt to trace the family any further. However, I do know that at least one of the above three named in the 1851 Census subsequently married and had children, and there may be descendants still living in the area today.

John Baguley's father, Joseph, had been a man of some means, as is proved from the details in his will. He was a victualler, almost certainly of the *Bell Inn* in Attenborough. It is sad to see how, over the fifty years following his death in 1793, the fortunes of his children suffered so badly. From being the son of a reasonably prosperous man, John became first a framework knitter, and then, probably as a result of the serious depression in that industry, a poor agricultural labourer. This illustrates only too well the terrible social conditions prevalent throughout the midland counties in the early 19th century, a time of much poverty and despair.

The Baguley family tree is shown as Appendix C and this should help to clarify the relationship of the various family members mentioned in this chapter.

A sketch of the Ghost House by local artist Mr W. Simpkins.
(Courtesy of Beeston & District Local History Society)

Field Lane at its junction with Ghost House Lane prior to residential development.
(Photo courtesy of Beeston & District Local History Society)

The same spot in 1998. (Photo, Steve Dance)

Looking down Ghost House Lane from Field Lane, 1998. (Photo, Steve Dance)

Looking down Ghost House Lane, 1998. (Photo, Steve Dance)

Looking up Ghost House Lane from Eskdale Drive, 1998. (Photo, Steve Dance)

The site of the Ghost House - corner of Valley Road and Pearson Avenue, 1998.
(Photo, Steve Dance)

The Ghost House in use as an apple store. The origin and date of this photograph are unknown. However, from the dress of the two gentlemen it is probably late 19th century. This view is of the back of the house, with the orchards behind the photographer.
(Photo, Nottinghamshire County Council Community Services)

Another old view of the Ghost House. Again, the date is unknown but probably late 19th
century. The similarity with the photograph opposite is clear and it is possible that both
photographs were taken at about the same time.
(Photo courtesy of Beeston & District Local History Society)

Ghost House Lane and the Ghost House. Date and origin of photograph unknown, but probably the early 1930s. It was clearly taken before the house was extended in the late 1930s. (Photo courtesy of Beeston & District Local History Society)

The same spot in 1998. The Ghost House stood on the site now occupied by the houses at the corner of Valley Road and Pearson Avenue. (Photo, Steve Dance)

The Ghost House, renamed Sunnyside Cottage, in 1946.
(Photo courtesy of Mrs Anne Robbins)

The Ghost House, from a watercolour painting by local artist Mr W. Simpkins.
Painted from memory approx. ten years after the house was demolished.
(Courtesy of Mr Roy Davies)

CHAPTER FIVE

WHO WAS THE PEDLAR? WHEN DID HE DIE?

When I set out to research the history of the Chilwell Ghost, I was fairly confident that I would be able to find out at least something about the alleged murderer of the pedlar; after all, I had been lucky enough to come across the 1888 item in the *Nottinghamshire Guardian* which named him. None of the other sources of written information on the subject had named John Baguley, and equally none had named the victim. But would it be possible to find out just who the pedlar was?

I was quite sure that the 1888 newspaper article must have been based on an earlier account, quite possibly one that had appeared at the time of John Baguley's death. I therefore started the tedious task of looking through various newspapers of the time. Many of these are available on microfilm, but anyone who has consulted these old newspapers will know just what a task it is! Unlike today's tabloids with their large print, short paragraphs and bold snappy headlines, the papers of 180 years ago were quite different; just column after column of tightly packed, extremely small type, much of it on matters of national and political interest, but also many others offering a fascinating glimpse of life at the time. Headlines, even where included, were equally small, and trying to find a report on a specific occurrence, particularly when there was no certainty that such a report had even appeared, was like looking for the proverbial 'needle in a haystack'.

Nevertheless, I started with the *Nottingham Journal*, one of a number of local weekly newspapers, published either on a Friday or Saturday. I knew that John Baguley had died on Friday 8th February 1850, so I first looked at the issue for Friday 15th February. Unable to find anything, I then looked at the following week's issue. One of the problems associated with looking at old newspapers, apart from eye strain, is that one can easily be distracted into reading other items of interest. Again, no luck, so on to the issue for Friday 1st March. Once more, after searching for some time nothing could be found, and I was just about to give up, when, out of the corner of my eye, two words suddenly leapt out of the page - **Chilwell Ghost**! What followed was the most detailed account I had yet found, and it had clearly been prompted by the recent death-bed confession of John Baguley. The story recounted the legend of the haunted house; how many years before a pedlar was supposed to have been murdered there and how subsequent happenings in the house had so alarmed the occupants and made Chilwell notorious in the area. But more importantly it gave a date for the supposed murder and it also named the victim - a certain Scotsman named McQuince.

I took a photocopy of the item then decided to see if any of the other newspapers had covered the story. I checked both the *Nottingham Review* and the *Nottingham Mercury*, and in both of their editions of 1st March found accounts.

All three carried broadly similar details, and that appearing in the *Nottingham Mercury* is shown opposite (this is the only one of the three of sufficient clarity to be reproduced). However, of the three accounts, that appearing in the *Nottingham Journal* was by far the most enlightening, as it contained some information not given in the other two, and also named some of the other characters in the story. Because this account is so interesting, it is transcribed here in full, exactly as it appeared (it will be noted that the name Baguley has here been spelt throughout as Bagguley):

THE NOTTINGHAM JOURNAL, MARCH 1ST 1850

EXTRAORDINARY AFFAIR - SUPPOSED DISCOVERY OF A MURDER

A startling event, which has occurred within the last few days, has formed the subject of much conversation within this district. For a considerable period anterior to the year 1827, a pedlar named McQuince, was in the habit of visiting this neighbourhood. He was a Scotchman and he dealt in drapery goods. It was his invariable custom, when at Chilwell, to make his last call at the Ash Flat House, the residence of one of Messrs. Pearson's men, a man named John Bagguley, and he was shrewdly suspected of matrimonial intentions towards the eldest girl. Bagguley's family, it may not be improper to state, consisted at that time, of three sons and two daughters, and considering the relative position of the parties the match was thought a capital one on the lady's side. One night towards the close of the year just named, he had been doing business with another of Messrs. Pearson's labourers, named Thomas Ballard, to whom he had succeeded in selling articles on credit to the amount of 18 shillings, and it being now very late, he asked leave to go by a short cut across an orchard to Bagguley's where he said he should sleep. The permission was immediately granted. He left Ballard's and has never been seen since. Ballard (who is still living) has never been called on for payment, nor have McQuince's other debtors, of whom there were, in Beeston and Chilwell, a rather large number. In about a year after his disappearance, a change for the better was noticed in the condition of the Bagguleys. He bought several pigs, and the cottage began to be more comfortably furnished. This raised various surmisings, and the neighbours began to compare notes. It was also remarked that the two girls wore new dresses of the same material, and a Mrs Boyd said they also gave her a piece to make a frock for her daughter. A man named Lees, stated that early on the morning after the pedlar had been seen last he felt an unaccountable and irresistible inclination to go to the Ash Flat House, and when he got thither (though it was before four o'clock) he

Extract from the Nottingham Mercury, dated 1st March 1850

CHILWELL.—*Confession of Murder.*—It has within the last two or three weeks been made known that John Baguley, aged 70, who died at Chilwell, four miles south of Nottingham, on the 16th ult., confessed on his deathbed, that 23 years ago, he murdered a hawker named Mac Quince, of shawls, blankets, &c., and disposed of the body. This announcement has caused the greatest possible excitement. From a preliminary investigation it seems that at the time stated, an individual of this description, suddenly disappeared, and all that could be learnt respecting him was that when last seen he was proceeding in the direction of Baguley's cottage. This and other incidents led to a suspicion that the Baguleys had made away with the missing man, which suspicion subsequent circumstances revived from time to time. At the period of his sudden disappearance the murdered man professed to be courting one of Baguley's daughters, and as he was known to be in possession of a considerable sum of money, he was looked upon as being a rather desirable suitor, especially as the Baguleys were known to be very poor. The hawker had not been missing more than 12 months, however, before their circumstances began to improve, and from the condition of a poverty-stricken labourer, Baguley became suddenly advanced to that of a comfortable cottager, with a number of pigs in his stye. This sudden improvement was coupled by the neighbours with the hawker's disappearance, and ever since the Baguleys have been looked upon with distrust. Two sons still living at Chilwell and another residing at a distance are supposed to have been cognizant of the foul transaction, although at the time of its occurrence they were very young; and that Baguley's first wife was, is certain, for whenever she quarrelled with her first husband, as she frequently did, she was in the habit of putting a stop to the violence of his temper by saying, "Be quiet, John; you know I have your coat of arms upstairs."— alluding to some bloody clothes that were supposed to be kept in a lodging room; she has also been heard to say to him, "you old wretch, I could hang you any day." The first Mrs. Baguley died five or six years ago, and said a short time previously, that she had something to reveal; but, this coming to her husband's knowledge, he never afterwards would allow a stranger to go into her room. The present Mrs. Baguley, now the widow of the murderer, was married to him about three years ago, since which time she says his conduct has been very strange. In his sleep frequently he would jump up in a state of great excitement and exclaim that some one was about to seize him. Three weeks before he died he said to her, "the pick that I killed the man with is in that dyke;" he then appeared to be insensible; and from that day to his death he would say no more on the subject. His widow further says "she has been at many deaths, but never with one whose countenance betrayed so much misery," nor could he ever bear to be alone. It is a singular fact that the cottage in which the murder is said to have been committed, has never since been occupied for any length of time, and in it periodically strange nocturnal noises are said to be heard. "The Chilwell ghost," and tales respecting "the haunted house at Chilwell," have during the last twenty years dismayed many thousands of persons residing within the locality. The whole of the above circumstances have been made known to Mr. T. B. Charlton, the local magistrate, and will, no doubt, be fully and officially investigated.

(By permission of the British Newspaper Library)

39

found Bagguley in his shirt sleeves at work in his garden. In 1837, Messrs. Pearson, knowing Bagguley to be of indifferent character, discharged him from the house, and put in another labourer in his place. The new comers had not been there long before they were alarmed one night, by a tremendous bang at the shutters. On going out to ascertain what was the matter, nothing could be seen. This was repeated, till the fame thereof spread throughout all the neighbouring district, for many miles around. It is described as being like the blow of something heavy, and of a certain degree of hardness - much indeed as would be caused by a large swede turnip thrown with considerable force against the shutters. Mr John Pearson went to the house twice, but as the knocking was heard neither time he was inclined to think it a clumsy trick. On a third occasion, however, he was more successful, and he was afterwards at some considerable pains to find out the supposed deception. His first suspicion was, that the player of the trick had thrown something against the shutter and drawn it away again; but on carefully inspecting the snow, not the slightest trace could be discovered; and this could hardly have been done. Mr Pearson also caused a trench to be dug all around the house, so as to discover any concealed wires. This failing, he had a frame made, a little larger than the window frame, and covered with blacked paper. This he fastened over the window at the distance of two or three inches from it. No sooner had it been put up and he had gone into the house, than the noise was heard. He rushed out, but the paper was not in the slightest degree injured. He then went upstairs into the room above, leaving some trustworthy persons to watch the inside of the shutter. While looking out of the window directly over the shutter (the night being light enough to see two or three fields off), bang! came the knock, fairly shaking the house; but still without damaging the screen. All the family at this time were at the other side of the room, so that they were not concerned in any hoax that it may be thought was practised. To proceed. Mr Pearson was now convinced that the mystery was inexplicable; and after promising without any result a handsome reward to the discoverer of the secret, he took no further steps. Another family was put into the house, but they meeting with the same annoyance, also left, and the building has since been used as an apple store. The above is the legend of the much talked of 'Chilwell Ghost', which during the winter of 1837/8 made in the midland counties full as great a sensation as that of Cock Lane did in London. Bagguley continued to live at Chilwell, but his wife died five or six years ago. She had been heard several times to say to her husband, when quarrelling with him, 'You know I could hang you any day - I've got your coat of arms up stairs.' Her neighbours sometimes asked her what she meant, and her answer was always 'He knows.' As her end drew nigh, she stated that she had something on her mind, which she should like to reveal, but her husband never afterwards admitted a stranger into the room, and so her evidence was lost. About three years since he married again, and his wife states that his conduct has been very strange. In his sleep he would frequently start up and exclaim that someone was about to seize him. His health had lately failed; and on the 15th inst. he said while in one of these fits, 'The pick is in the brook.' His wife asked 'What pick?' 'That pick, that pick!' was the reply. After this he gradually grew worse, and on the next day he suddenly sprung up. His eyes rolled fearfully, and he made motions as if he saw some spectacle of horror. His attendant and his wife, who had become quite convinced of his guilt, fled in affright, and when they mustered courage to return, which they did in a few minutes after, they found that he had ceased to breathe. Conscience had done her work. No one can recount the terrors of that solitary chamber: for there was no witness but Heaven to the awful struggle in which the soul of the murderer tore itself from the crime - stained body, and stood before its Judge! Search has been made for the pick, but we believe it has not yet been successful. Bagguley was 70 years of age, his daughters are dead, but his sons still survive.

It seems clear that the article which appeared in the *Nottinghamshire Guardian* in 1888 (see page 17), had been based on the newspaper reports of 1850. It was also likely that these reports, following John Baguley's death-bed confession to the murder, reawakened interest in the Chilwell Ghost and resulted in the publication of the Rhymed Account (see Chapter 3). The *Nottingham Journal* report of 1st March 1850 is significant in that it provides much more information than can be found in the other reports, in particular the name of the pedlar and the date of the supposed murder - late in 1827. However, it does contain a few errors which were perpetuated in the 1888 article, in particular the date of John Baguley's death (quoted as the 16th, rather than the 8th February) and his age (70 instead of 61).

There are also a few other minor errors; the report states that Baguley had three sons and two daughters, whereas he actually had two sons and three daughters, although it is correct in stating that all his daughters had predeceased him. The report also confirms that it was Baguley's eldest daughter, Diana, who had formed a liaison with McQuince, which is not surprising - in 1827 she was aged about 16, whilst Maria was about 13 and Jane only 8. Three names are also given which are not to be found in the other newspaper reports. The last man allegedly to see the pedlar before he set off for the Ash Flat House was a Thomas Ballard, who was said to be still living in 1850. As stated earlier, Ballard was a common name in the Chilwell and Attenborough area - John's father's first wife was a Mary Ballard.

The man who was said to have walked over to the Ash Flat House and found Baguley digging his garden early one morning (described as a former parish constable in Mellor's account of 1919), is here named as Lees (or possibly Lee); and the neighbour of Baguley's who is stated to have been given some of the pedlar's material is named as a Mrs Boyd.

I checked the 1841 and 1851 Census returns and was able to find probable references to all these persons. In 1841, a Thomas Ballard, FWK, was living at Chilwell South

Side, aged between 45 and 50, with his wife and six children. By 1851, his wife had died but he was still living in Chilwell with one of his sons, aged 56 and still a FWK.

No forename was given in the newspaper account for the man named Lees, but there were three persons who might be the one named. Two men named William Lee appear in the 1841 Census, both living at Attenborough, aged about 60 and 65 and one Thomas Lee aged about 55. By 1851, the elder William Lee had died but the other was still living at Attenborough, aged 76 a 'Chelsea Pensioner and FWK'. Of Thomas Lee no trace could be found.

For the name Boyd, only one family was to be found. In 1841, a Harriet Boyd was living at Chilwell South Side, a seamstress, aged about 35, along with five children aged between 4 and 15. There was no reference to her husband, but she is almost certainly Harriet Burdett of Chilwell who had married George Boyd at Bramcote on 22nd August 1824 'with parents consent', indicating that either or both were under 21. And guess who was living next door to Mrs Boyd in 1841 - none other than John Baguley and his family - see page 24 for a copy of the census entry.

By the time of the 1851 Census she had moved and was living in Cow Lane, Bramcote, now a laundress aged 45, and three of her children were still living with her. In 1827, when the murder allegedly took place, she would have been about 21, and could therefore be the Mrs Boyd who used some of the material to 'make a frock for her daughter'. Although in neither the 1841 nor the 1851 Census returns was there a girl old enough to have been alive in 1827, a Mary Boyd of Chilwell was buried at Attenborough on 5th May 1838, aged 14 and this is likely to have been the daughter referred to, born shortly after her parents had married.

The *Nottingham Journal* account also confirms what had already been discovered in the census returns for 1841 - that the Baguley family had by that time left the Ash Flat House. This account even gives the date when they were, in effect, evicted - 1837. It was only after the next family had moved into the Ash Flat House that the strange happenings were first reported to the landlord, Mr Pearson.

The next chapter discusses in more detail the actual haunting. The reference to 'Cock Lane in London' refers to a famous poltergeist case which occurred at a house in Cock Lane in 1760.

Whilst the *Nottingham Journal's* account was, overall, probably the most comprehensive, there were two interesting statements made in the *Nottingham Review's* account which do not appear in the other two. Firstly, it was stated that John Baguley, in his final illness, was attended by a Mr Butler, a surgeon from Beeston. The relevant section reads as follows:

42

. . . He died on the 16th inst. when labouring under an attack of paralysis, and it has been very generally said that he had made some important disclosures to Mr Butler, surgeon, of Beeston, who attended him. This is entirely without foundation, for not a word passed between that gentleman and Baguley of an extraordinary nature. During his fits of insensibility, however, the sick man frequently made strange ejaculations such as 'Oh that pick with which I murdered the packman' and very shortly before death, he said, in the hearing of his wife, 'The pick that I killed the packman with I buried in the dyke.'

James Butler was a member of the Royal College of Surgeons. Originally from Ireland, he was for many years the doctor in Beeston. He died in 1893 aged 75 and is commemorated by a window in the south aisle of Beeston Parish Church, depicting Peter and John healing the cripple at the Beautiful Gate (Acts 3).

The other statement was as follows:

. . . Immediately after the murder, search was made round about the cottage for the body of McQuince, but it could not be found. Some parties seem still of opinion that his remains might still be brought to light if another more rigorous search were to be instituted, and we hear that application will be made to the authorities of the place for that purpose. The 'Haunted House' is on the estate of Messrs. Pearson, nurserymen, of Chilwell, and is now used by them as a store for apples, Baguley having left it some years since.

It appears then, that following John Baguley's death-bed confession to the murder, a search was made for the body, but without success. Mr A. L. Searle (see page 4) claimed that his grandfather had been present when bones were found. However, it seems certain that there was never an official investigation, despite the above report's statement that '. . . *application will be made to the authorities of the place for that purpose.*' If a proper inquiry had been carried out, this would surely have been widely reported, especially if any remains had been found.

These newspaper accounts from 1850 have therefore provided considerable details not shown elsewhere. The most important facts given here are the approximate date of the murder (late 1827) and the identity of the pedlar - a Scotsman by the name of McQuince. This is a most unusual name, so there was always a hope that it might be possible to find out more about him. Unfortunately, no other facts were quoted; no forename was given nor his age or where he lived. It is likely that, being a pedlar, he had no fixed abode and simply relied on the kind hospitality of his customers to provide him with a bed for the night - a practice which was eventually to lead to his death. However, without additional information other than his surname, the search for more details was to prove very difficult. If he had no close relations he might not have been reported missing, and there were no earlier census returns to check for him. Trying to find entries in parish registers would be a daunting task as it was not known where he came from, when he was born or who his parents were.

I therefore turned to the IGI (International Genealogical Index). This is a worldwide index containing entries from parish registers, compiled by the Church of Latter Day Saints (the Mormons) and stored at Utah. It is available on microfiche and can be found in many record offices and local studies libraries. The British version is divided into counties, with names appearing in alphabetical order of surname, then forename, then in chronological order. It shows baptisms and marriages (but not burials) and is a very quick way of looking at a particular name in any county. However, it is not complete as not every parish has been included, and even for those that are included there are some omissions and errors.

Nevertheless, despite its shortcomings it is still a very valuable tool in trying to trace records of baptisms and marriages, and also in checking the geographical distribution of any specific surname. It is now also available on a computer database, so that one can search for a name and all entries for that name will be listed for the whole country. This facility is especially useful if one is trying to find entries for a particular name where the county of residence is not known. I searched this database for the name McQuince (or MacQuince). The result - a total blank. For the whole of the British Isles, there was not one single entry for this surname. There were plenty of persons named Quince, Quincey, Quinn, McQuinn, McQueen and other similar variations, but not for McQuince.

As indicated above, the IGI is neither 100% complete nor accurate, but the fact that there are no references for the name McQuince indicates that it is a very rare name. Perhaps it was not the pedlar's real name, but merely the name by which he was known to the folks of the area; maybe it was a nickname or an alias. Possibly, because he was a Scotsman, the locals had added the prefix 'Mc' or 'Mac' to his name, which might have been plain Quince. The problem is that without a clue to start a search it will be very difficult to find any more about him. Apart from parish records, there are few sources to check, especially for someone who may not have been a property owner. What is required is a stroke of luck. It is still possible that some other record may one day be uncovered which might lead us to find out more about him - where he came from, when he was born and whether he left any relatives.

But until then we shall simply have to be content with what little we know, based on the newspaper reports - that the pedlar, who is central to the whole of this story, was a Scotsman by the name of McQuince.

CHAPTER SIX

THE HAUNTING

We have now discovered in some detail the facts surrounding the alleged murder of the pedlar. We know his name, even if we know little more of this unfortunate character. We know who was living at the Ash Flat House at the time the pedlar disappeared and we have found out much about John Baguley and his family.

But what of the actual haunting? For this was the event which really put Chilwell on the map, and, if contemporary reports are to be believed, caused thousands of people to flock to the village and to the Ash Flat House in the hopes of a glimpse of 'something'.

The murder, if indeed a murder did take place, is supposed to have happened late in 1827, but it was to be another ten years before stories of strange happenings at the Ash Flat House began to circulate in the locality. The accounts which appeared in the local newspapers in March 1850 following John Baguley's death-bed confession of the murder, make it clear that it was not until late in 1837 that the first reports of strange happenings were conveyed to Mr Pearson, the owner of the Ash Flat House. As the *Nottingham Journal* reported:

In 1837, Messrs. Pearson, knowing Bagguley to be of indifferent character, discharged him from the house, and put in another labourer in his place. The new comers had not been there long before they were alarmed one night, by a tremendous bang at the shutters . . .

The implication is clearly that it was **not** the Baguley family which reported the strange happenings, but the new family which had been installed there. But then, if anything strange had been experienced by the Baguleys, the last thing they would have wanted was to draw attention to themselves, especially if they had murdered McQuince. It is my belief that, quite possibly, nothing strange had been experienced until the new family moved in, and the likely explanation for this is discussed later in this chapter. The *Nottingham Review* of 1st March 1850 had explained in some detail the nature of the happenings, and the steps taken by John Pearson to try and find out the cause. This part of the report concludes:

. . . . The above is the legend of the much talked of 'Chilwell Ghost' which during the winter of 1837/8 made in the midland counties full as great a sensation as that of Cock Lane did in London . . . .

If this was so, and the story was such a sensation, then hopefully it might be possible to find some contemporary newspaper accounts. So, once again, a long and tedious search began of local newspapers published during the winter of 1837/38. Eventually, I struck lucky and found a short report in the *Nottingham Journal* edition of Friday 26th January 1838. This reads as follows:

A Ghost ! - The village of Chilwell has for some time been kept in a state of agitation by a rumour that some supernatural knockings are heard at the cottage of a labourer. This report has drawn crowds of visitors night after night, to the haunted spot, but still this ghost re-visits, as Hamlet says 'the glimpses of the moon, making night hideous'. Some swear, and some pray; but despite both blasphemy and devotion, the nocturnal disturber continues his mysterious, and as our deponent saith, inexplicable rappings of the shutters of the dwelling - though every effort has been made to discover the 'whereabouts' of the intruder, and to prevent trickery. We suppose that, ere long, as in most other similar cases, the mystery will be solved, and prove the truth of the adage 'one fool makes many'.

Their reporter was clearly sceptical as to the reality of the happenings! Having discovered this account, I looked at other newspapers for about the same time, and soon found that the events had also been reported in the *Nottingham Review*.

Their account, which also appeared on 26th January 1838 was slightly more detailed, and of more significance was the fact that it named the new family which had lately moved into the Ash Flat House. It reads as follows:

. . . . If we had been disposed to excite the interest of that portion of our readers who are prone to the marvellous, or to have pandered to the vitiated taste of credulity and superstition, we should some weeks since have noticed, an extraordinary visitation, which continues to be the object of deep attention to those who admit the belief of supernatural agency, and of rational research to others who are desirous to investigate truth and dispel delusion. A very secluded spot, situated in the fields between the villages of Chilwell and Bramcote, and the residence of a cottager of the name of Adcock, has been for some time the nightly resort of great numbers, attracted by violent concussions, at irregular intervals, on the outside of one of the shutters of the lower part of the dwelling. These concussions have been heard at all periods from night-fall until morning, when the family have been alone, and when numbers have been present within and on all sides of the dwelling. Watchmen have been set for a considerable circuit round, and a false shutter of paper has been placed over the one from which the noise is heard, but hitherto every attempt to discover the origin of the concussions, or the mode of producing them has entirely failed. In thus noticing the transaction, we ought in justice to add that there is nothing in the character or deportment of the family to justify any suspicion of privity

or connivance, and a total absence of every apparent motive for this continued interruption of all domestic peace and tranquillity.

The *Review's* reporter appears less sceptical, and specifically exonerates the Adcock family from any accusation of fraudulent activity. He also describes the attempts made to find the cause of the noises, as described in much more detail by Robert Mellors in his book of 1919.

The *Nottingham Review* states '. . . *we should some weeks since have noticed, an extraordinary visitation . . .*' whilst the *Nottingham Journal* states '. . . *the village of Chilwell has for some time been kept in a state of agitation by a rumour that some supernatural knockings are heard at the cottage of a labourer . . .*'

This seems to imply that the strange happenings had commenced a short time prior to the reports appearing in the newspapers. Despite an extensive search through the newspaper files from October 1837 onwards, the above are the first reports I have found of the Chilwell Ghost, and from the way they are written, I believe them to be the first accounts to appear. Had there been any earlier accounts, these would almost certainly have been referred to.

It would appear, therefore, that the noises at the Ash Flat House had probably started late in 1837, which was about the same time that the Baguleys had been moved out and the new family, whom we now know to be named Adcock, moved in.

What exactly was it about the Baguleys that suddenly caused Mr Pearson to evict them? The *Nottingham Journal* stated that he considered Baguley to be of 'indifferent character'. There had, of course, been rumours in the village for almost ten years that he had murdered the pedlar. And his daughter Diana had given birth to three illegitimate children. Illegitimacy was not as unusual in the 19th century as many people might believe, and it was quite common for the first child of a marriage to arrive well under nine months after the date of the wedding. However, for a girl to have three illegitimate children and never to marry was somewhat unusual, and it can be imagined that her behaviour must have caused a degree of critical comment in the village. And then there was the little matter of Diana's appearance at Nottingham Crown Court.

In undertaking historical research, much time can be spent in a long slow search for documentary evidence, but very occasionally one strikes lucky, and quite by accident comes across information which proves to be of great significance.

Whilst searching through the columns of the *Nottingham Mercury* for accounts of the Chilwell haunting, I could hardly believe my luck when I unexpectedly came across another item in which the name Baguley featured prominently. Then, as now, newspapers carried accounts of local court cases.

The Michaelmas Quarter Sessions were taking place at Nottingham in October/November 1837, and the *Mercury's* edition of Saturday 4th November carried an extensive report of all the current court proceedings, listing the judge, jury and details of all the cases heard. Amongst these cases was the following:

Nottingham Michaelmas Quarter Sessions. Crown Court Friday 3rd November

Diana Baguley aged 26 and Jane Baguley aged 18 to stealing from the shop of James Farmer and partner on 28th October last, 15 yards of green silk velvet, and a quantity of other silks and mercery. A second indictment charged them with stealing, on the same day, from the shop of Jacob Forth, a hat and three lamb skins. To which Diana Baguley pleaded guilty and Jane Baguley not guilty. Diana six months hard labour in the House of Correction, Jane three months hard labour in the House of Correction.

A case of 'like father like daughter' perhaps. Maybe stealing material ran in the family, but at least the girls did not commit murder in the course of their robbery! Various Trade Directories of the time show that James Farmer was a linen and woollen draper who had a shop on South Parade, Nottingham. Also on South Parade was Jacob Forth, furrier and hatter.

The House of Correction, Nottingham.

48

Unfortunately, the details of the court case do not include the address of the accused, nor whether they were related. However, it is reasonable to assume they were related and most likely sisters. Whilst there were a few other families by the name of Baguley in Nottinghamshire, I am quite certain that the two girls here mentioned are the daughters of John Baguley. Their ages fit exactly, and the chance of there being two other sisters of the same name and ages is remote. I spent some time checking a number of other sources to see whether I could find two other sisters named Diana and Jane Baguley of the right age, but without success. Indeed, there was only one Diana and one Jane Baguley that fitted - the daughters of John Baguley of Chilwell.

The sisters' appearance in court and subsequent sentence to hard labour must have been the talk of the village. Perhaps this was the 'straw that broke the camel's back' and John Pearson decided that enough was enough and that the Baguleys must go. This would have put the date of their eviction, and the Adcocks' move to the Ash Flat House, at about November 1837, two months before the newspapers carried the first accounts of the haunting.

We now need to look in some detail at the actual haunting itself. The various reports all agree to a very great extent as to the nature of the haunting. It consisted, almost entirely, of loud knocks or rappings on the shutters, but the *Nottingham Guardian* article of 1888 also referred to groans, taps and cups and saucers rattling. However, so far as I know, there are no reports of any apparition. In short, this was a clear case of poltergeist activity.

One could write volumes and debate for ever the case for and against the existence of ghosts and the reality of poltergeist phenomena. Indeed, numerous books can be found on the subject, but this is not the place to join in that particular debate. For anyone not familiar with the subject, it will suffice to explain briefly what is involved. The classic ghost haunting will normally consist of the appearance, from time to time, of the apparition of a dead person. The haunting will normally occur at a location where that person lived and, most likely, died. Often the person whose ghost is seen may have died in tragic circumstances.

Poltergeist activity, whilst often classified under the same general heading of 'haunting' is believed by many to be nothing to do with ghosts, although in the past such incidents were thought to be the work of the spirits of the dead. The word poltergeist is Germanic in origin, meaning noisy, or mischievous (polter), and ghost (geist). The commonest features of poltergeist activity include knockings and rappings, sometimes extremely violent, and the movement of objects by no apparent physical means. Other features include the disappearance of objects, followed some time later by their equally mysterious reappearance; showers of stones falling onto houses; voices; writing on walls, and even the outbreak of fires. These phenomena can last anything from a few days up to several years. It is now generally accepted that in most poltergeist cases there is one particular person whose presence seems to be necessary for the phenomena to be triggered, the so called 'focus' of the phenomena.

This focus is usually someone at the age of puberty, more often a girl, and is usually aware that their presence is causing the phenomena, without being able to prevent it. It is almost as if an invisible 'energy' is emanating from the person, which finds an outlet in the form of noises, the movement of objects etc. The focus is often someone who has been the victim of circumstances resulting in anxiety, possibly having suffered some trauma or upset.

In comparison with many of the most famous poltergeist cases, the Chilwell affair appears, by all accounts, to have been fairly low-key. There are no reports of the more spectacular kind of incidents, and had these occurred it is almost certain that they would have been reported. There are no accounts of showers of stones falling on the Ash Flat House, nor of objects moving of their own volition. However, what is clear is that there were some quite violent knockings on the shutters. We are fortunate that the landlord, John Pearson, took such a personal interest in the case, even to the extent of carrying out some admirable amateur investigations to try and detect the cause of the noises, and to trap any would-be trickster - but without success.

We also know that these events were only reported after the Adcock family had moved into the Ash Flat House. Could one of that family have been the focus for the knockings? And if so, had similar phenomena occurred at their previous home, or their subsequent home? In some poltergeist cases it has been reported that the phenomena have occurred wherever the person concerned went.

In a famous poltergeist case at Sauchie in Scotland, which happened in late 1960/61, the centre of the activity was an eleven-year-old girl, Virginia Campbell. The classic knockings, rappings and movements of objects occurred not only at her home, but also in her school classroom. And Matthew Manning, now a well-known medium, had been at the centre of many strange occurrences as a teenager, not only at his home but also at his boarding school.

The next step was to try and find whether the Adcock family included someone who might have been the focus. Using the same sources that I had used to trace details of the Baguley family, I did the same for the Adcocks. Both the 1841 and 1851 Census returns show that there were only two families of that name living in Chilwell, that of William Adcock and his family, and another William Adcock, the latter being the eldest son of the former.

The 1851 Census even names the two Williams as 'senior' and 'junior' (it is quite unusual for this distinction to be shown in census returns). From the information gathered in the census returns and the local parish registers, it was possible to draw up a picture of the two Adcock families as they must have existed in 1837/38.

William Adcock (senior) was born about 1796, and on 13th October 1815 he married Sarah Johnson at Attenborough. She was a year younger than William, and the records indicate that they had at least eleven children. Whilst it has not been possible to establish the exact dates of their birth, the following is fairly accurate:

William born 1815/16; George born 1817/18; Frances born 1820 (died April 1822); Jonathan born and died July 1821; Elizabeth born 1822/23; Eliza born 1825/26; David born May 1828; Sarah born August 1831; Jonathan born April 1833; Elija born about 1830 and Emma born about 1837.

William Adcock (junior) married Hannah Mather at Barrow upon Trent on 8th December 1834, and their first child, Sarah, was baptised at Barrow upon Trent on 4th January 1835. They had at least six more children: William born 1836/37; George born 1838/39; Elizabeth born 1841; Jeffrey born 1842/43; James born 1845/46 and Ann born 1848/49.

As stated earlier, census returns did not give actual addresses, but they did indicate that both families were living in Chilwell South, i.e. south of the Turnpike Road, and not, therefore, at the Ash Flat House. It is also not known which of the two Adcock families was moved into the Ash Flat House in 1837, but it seems they did not stay for long, and had certainly moved out by the time of the 1841 Census. As the *Nottingham Mercury* had stated:

. . . . *Mr Pearson was now convinced that the mystery was inexplicable; and after promising without any result a handsome reward to the discoverer of the secret, he took no further steps. Another family was put into the house, but they meeting with the same annoyance, also left, and the building has since been used as an apple store.*

Could it perhaps, after all, be the case that there really was something strange or abnormal about the Ash Flat House which was just waiting for the right 'focus' to be present for the extraordinary events to start happening? Could the restless spirit of the murdered pedlar be present, as was so widely believed by many in the locality? In his book *Can we explain the Poltergeist?* A.R.G. Owen examines the three classic theories of the nature of the poltergeist: whether it is a discarnate entity acting independently of the focus; an entity requiring a focus in order to operate; or purely a paranormal extension of the focus.

At the time of the haunting, it seems that most of the locals believed in the first of these possibilities, i.e. that the noises were caused by the spirit of the murdered pedlar. But if this was the case, why did the rappings only start ten years after the murder? Unless of course the Baguleys had experienced similar phenomena but had deliberately kept quiet.

The second theory, the 'mediumistic' theory of poltergeists, would explain why the phenomena only occurred at the Ash Flat House, assuming that one of the Adcock family was the focus. If one is inclined to believe the third theory, then the haunting had nothing whatsoever to do with the alleged murder of the pedlar, and the fact that these two events happened at the same place would, therefore, be purely coincidental.

Poltergeist cases are certainly a fascinating subject and anyone who is interested is recommended to study it further. As to the true explanation for such events, readers must make up their own minds.

If one favours the theory that a pubescent girl or boy is normally present for the poltergeist activity to begin, then it would seem more likely that it was William senior and his family who were living there. In 1837/38, assuming that all his children were still alive and living at home (except William junior who was by then married), his household would have included George aged 21, Elizabeth 15, Eliza 12, David 9, Sarah 6, Jonathan 4, Elija 2 and Emma 1.

It is probable that Elizabeth may actually have died as a child (although I have been unable to find any record in the local parish registers of the burial of Elizabeth Adcock) since she does not appear in the 1841 Census and their next daughter was baptised Eliza. It would be unusual to use two variations of the same name, unless the first child had already died. (Their son Jonathan had died within a day or two of being born and they subsequently named another son Jonathan).

According to the newspaper reports, after the Adcock family left the Ash Flat House another family moved in. Unfortunately, I have been unable, so far, to establish the name of this second family. Again, according to these reports, they also witnessed these disturbing events and, like the Adcocks, left the Ash Flat House.

Such are the details it has been possible to find about the actual haunting. Presumably, once the house ceased to be used as a residence, accounts of strange happenings would begin to die down. But clearly the Ash Flat House had by now acquired a reputation as a haunted house, and forever after it would be known locally as the Ghost House.

CHAPTER SEVEN

THE GHOST HOUSE IN LATER YEARS

At some stage following all the excitement, the house was turned into an apple store. Again, we do not know the actual date when the second family moved out, but we can guess that it may not have been too long after they moved in. Mr Pearson, understandably, did not want hundreds of sightseers tramping over his orchards, and he may have decided that the best option was to bring the saga to a conclusion by moving out the inhabitants, thus ending any continued stories of a ghost.

There is the claim in Robert Mellor's account that an old cobbler occupied the Ghost House for a year and also experienced the noises. If this is true, then it would tend to give credence to those who believe the pedlar's ghost was the culprit. Unfortunately, no other corroborative evidence has been found to support the story about the cobbler, nor of the date that he was supposed to have lived there. It is quite likely that the house was inhabited from time to time, and as we shall see shortly, it was indeed inhabited again from about 1938 to 1952.

But there is a clue in the 1851 Census to indicate that the house was, by then, uninhabited. As already explained, in rural areas houses tended not to be numbered or named at that time, so it is often difficult to identify particular houses in the census with those shown on a map. However, adjacent houses are listed sequentially in the census return. Overleaf is a copy of a page from this census for Chilwell, north of the Turnpike Road, which included Field Lane, Ghost House Lane, the Ash Flat House and 'Whitegrasses' - now known as Wheatgrass Farm. This shows that next to George Jackson, a gamekeeper, were two uninhabited houses, then the next inhabited house was Whitegrasses, the property of Thomas Purseglove, a farmer.

An examination of the maps reproduced on pages 8 and 9 shows that halfway along Field Lane was a cottage; this was 'Keeper's Cottage', home of the gamekeeper. Between there and Whitegrasses one would have walked along Field Lane, turned right, past the Ash Flat House and up the hill to Whitegrasses. The Chilwell Estate map of 1829 shows only three other buildings, a small one just beyond the end of Ghost House Lane, the Ash Flat House itself and then another, more substantial building in the corner of the field numbered 19. The two uninhabited houses mentioned in the census return most likely included the Ash Flat House as one of these.

1851 Census. HO 107 / 2141 Folio 88 Page 7
Chilwell - north of Turnpike Road

It is likely then, from the accounts we have, that the Ghost House probably became uninhabited sometime in the early 1840s. Unfortunately, the 1841 Census contains far less detail than that of 1851, and it has not been possible to deduce from it whether the Ash Flat House was inhabited at that time.

The house probably remained as an apple store for many years thereafter. In 1892, Messrs. Pearsons decided to sell much of their property in the Chilwell area and an auction was held on Wednesday 23rd November that year at the Mart, Bridlesmith Gate, Nottingham.

A total of 21 lots was put up for sale, and lot 10 was the Ash Flat. The following is reproduced from the sale document:

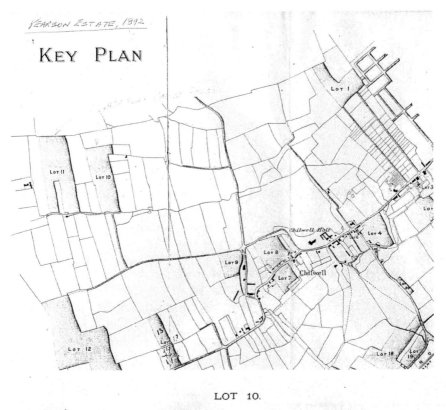

LOT 10.

A PIECE of valuable PASTURE LAND, used as an Orchard, with the Building thereon used as an Apple Shed, known by the name of the Ash Flat, and containing an area of 11a. 2r. 29p.

(Reproduced courtesy of Mr Roy Davies)

55

This also confirms that the Ghost House was then in use as an apple shed. This lot was sold for £625 to William Hollingsworth. The Hollingsworths are an old Chilwell family, still well represented in the area. Until recently they had a dairy and fruit and vegetable business, delivering both round the village. William himself died on 30th November 1952, just about the time that the Ghost House was being demolished. For the first third of the 20th century, the Ghost House stood empty in its lonely spot, standing out in the fields above the village, and used as an apple store or for other agricultural purposes. No doubt the children of the village would visit it, daring their friends to go inside, if this was possible, and perhaps vying with each other to tell the most lurid tales imaginable of the ghost of the murdered pedlar.

Then, in about 1938 it once more became a home, when the Robbins family moved from Chard in Somerset to Chilwell, Mr Robbins having secured a position with Messrs. Bartons of Sunnyside Farm, who by then owned the house and surrounding land. The old Ghost House was opened up again and the Robbins family lived there until it was demolished. Mrs Robbins didn't like the name 'Ghost House' and changed its name to 'Sunnyside Cottage'. It appears under this name on the 1939 version of the 25 inch O.S. map.

The Robbins family was large, there being ten children, and because of this and the small size of the Ghost House, an extension was added. This virtually doubled its size, and the height of the gable was increased at its apex. The photograph on page 35 was taken in about 1946 by Mr Alfred Robbins, and his wife Anne can just be seen standing at the front door. A comparison between this photograph and the earlier photographs makes it clear how the house was altered.

Alfred was one of the ten children of the Robbins family and was born in 1920. After the family moved to Chilwell he met, and eventually married Anne Slater. She was born in 1915 and lived with her parents in Worksop, but in 1941 had moved to Chilwell to work as a land army girl on Sunnyside Farm. It was during her time there that she met her future husband. Anne and Alfred were married in August 1946 and later that year they moved into the Ghost House with their in-laws. There were four bedrooms in the now enlarged house, and they had one of the bedrooms in the old part, the room where, some say, the pedlar was murdered.

Mrs Robbins said that she loved living in the old Ghost House, despite the fact that it was in such a lonely spot, and a considerable walk to the nearest shops! She was fully aware of its history, and that the pedlar was supposed to have been murdered there, but despite this has described it as a very happy house. She never felt frightened, nor did she experience any of the disturbing happenings which the Adcock family had suffered from over a hundred years earlier.

However, she revealed that she did have one very strange experience there. One day when she was alone in the house, she was kneeling down on the floor clearing out the ashes from the hearth, when she clearly felt as if a hand had been placed on her shoulder. She turned round quickly, thinking that one of the boys from the farm was playing a trick, but there was no one there. When she later told her mother-in-law what had happened, she admitted that she too had had exactly the same experience whilst cleaning out the grate.

Anne and Alfred moved out of the Ghost House in June 1949 to a council house on nearby Sunnyside Road, as they now had two young children, but felt sad to leave. The remainder of the family stayed there until about 1952/53 when they had to leave as it was to be demolished to make way for an extension to the Inham Nook housing estate. On the day of their move, it was Alfred who locked the door for the last time.

In 1998 Mrs Robbins was still living in Chilwell, and I went with her to see what she could remember of the location where she had spent such a happy time. She explained that the house was approached from the bottom of Ghost House Lane, at the point where it turned sharp left to run parallel with the brook. The house stood about thirty yards to the right, where there was a little wooden footbridge across the brook, and a path to the front door. There was a small hedge, separating the front garden from the brook. Behind the house was the large orchard with many fruit trees.

Although unable to be precise, Mrs Robbins thought that the actual site of the Ghost House is now occupied by the houses near the corner of Valley Road and Pearson Avenue (see photograph on page 31). This confirmed what I had already deduced by a comparison of old and new maps and local council plans made at the time of the extension to the housing estate.

Much has now altered; the brook has vanished into pipes underground and the former orchards are covered with houses. However, the little copse of trees which stood across the lane from the brook and house is still there, next to Eskdale Drive and Eskdale School.

In the early 1960s, further building work started on Field Lane itself. The 1963 Electoral Register shows just three new houses on Field Lane; the following year about 24 are shown and by 1965 building work was virtually complete. The whole surrounding area is now a pleasant residential area. Where previously there had been fields and orchards there are now new roads, houses and flats.

Interestingly, Ghost House Lane still remains as a footpath off Field Lane, bounded by its original hedges, and still looking much as it always did (see the photographs on page 30). However, it is now somewhat shorter than it was formerly. A new road,

Eskdale Drive, cuts across it near the bottom and Ghost House Lane continues as a named footpath to where it meets Valley Road. This junction marks the point where the lane originally turned sharp left to run alongside the brook.

I am also indebted to Mr Peter Hiley of Spondon, Derby, for supplying some details and drawings of the house as it was both before and after the alterations that took place in the late 1930s. The sketches and plans which follow were done by Mr Alfred Robbins for Mr Hiley in 1985, when he was undertaking a project about the Ghost House for the Barncroft Day Centre. Mr Hiley's own sketch of how the Ghost House might have looked in the 19th century is also shown.

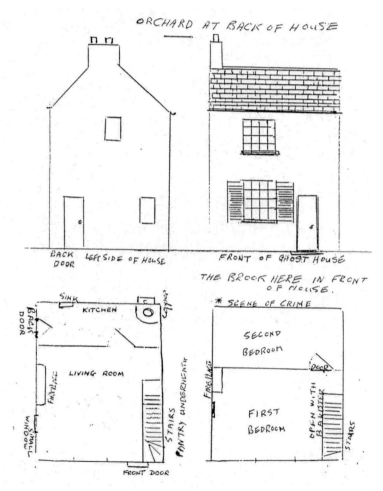

Sketches showing the layout of the Ghost House made by Mr Alfred Robbins, who lived there with his family from about 1938 to 1949.

58

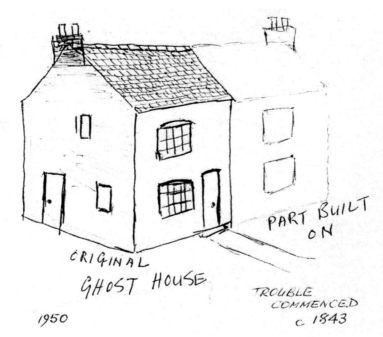

A sketch of the Ghost House made by Mr Alfred Robbins.

Peter Hiley's drawing of the Ghost House as it probably appeared in the 19th century.

CHAPTER EIGHT

CONCLUSIONS

Our trail of discovery has unearthed many facts about the legend of the Chilwell Ghost. We now know, within a month or two, when the events took place and we know the names of the main characters. Indeed, we now know quite a lot about the Baguley family in particular. Of the pedlar, the supposed victim, it has not been possible to find out a great deal. We know his name but little else.

The two principal questions in the whole saga are, of course: Did a murder actually take place? Was the Ash Flat House really haunted?

The second of these two questions is probably the easier to answer, if only because it is the sort of question which can never be answered to everyone's satisfaction. Some people simply do not accept the reality of the so called 'supernatural'. For them, there will always be a rational explanation for any phenomena which might occur, and no amount of evidence will ever convince them otherwise. Equally, many people are willing to accept that there may be occasions when strange phenomena occur which we are not able to explain.

I think that it is not really important to try and prove this point one way or another. In setting out to investigate the legend of the Chilwell Ghost, it was never my intention to try and do this. I merely wanted to discover more about the *legend itself* - to put flesh onto the bare bones of the story, to find out when these events took place and the names of the people involved; to discover a little more about them and their families, how and where they lived. In this, I like to think I have succeeded, although I am sure there is still more to be discovered.

The fact remains however, (and this cannot be denied even by even the staunchest sceptic) that in the 19th century, many people *did* believe that the Ash Flat House was haunted; strange noises were reported and were investigated by the landlord, but he was unable to come up with a satisfactory explanation.

Undoubtedly there would have been some wild stories circulating in the area, and no doubt some equally gross exaggerations will have occurred in the telling. It is also true to say that country people were probably less sophisticated and more superstitious 170 years ago than they are today, and more willing to accept at face value what they were told. Had these events been happening today, then no doubt psychic researchers would have been on hand to undertake some more serious research into the alleged manifestations, as has happened in more recent cases.

And what about the alleged murder of the pedlar. Did this really happen? This question is more difficult to answer with any degree of certainty. Unfortunately, no investigation took place at the time, which is a pity, as it might have unearthed the truth, literally, had the garden of the Ash Flat House been dug up!

If McQuince was murdered by Baguley, then what was the motive? It is assumed that he was murdered simply for his money and possessions, and there is no doubt that to a poor agricultural labourer these would be tempting. But would they be tempting enough to commit murder? There were many poor people living at the time, but this did not result in an outbreak of murder. Could there, then, have been another motive? It is a well-known fact that the majority of murders tend to be domestic in their cause, often committed in the heat of the moment. It was rumoured that John Baguley's daughter, Diana, was romantically involved with the pedlar. If this was so, could this have had something to do with the murder? McQuince, in view of his relative wealth, might have appeared an attractive catch for Diana, and her father might well have been keen for a marriage to take place.

But there may have been some friction which sparked an argument - perhaps McQuince had promised to marry Diana but had then changed his mind, or maybe Baguley had caught his daughter and McQuince behaving a little too amorously for his liking, for subsequent events proved that Diana was not exactly the most virtuous young lady in Chilwell! We shall never know, but it is interesting to speculate what exactly caused Baguley, that fateful night late in 1827, to take an axe and murder the pedlar, as the legend tells us happened.

Whatever the cause of the murder might have been, once the act was committed it would have been necessary to dispose of the body, and to hide McQuince's possessions. His money and his goods could have been hidden away for some time, but the temptation would eventually have become too great not to take advantage of them. The money would have been used to improve their household effects, and to purchase some pigs, as was reported, and the material used to provide the girls with new dresses. The most likely hiding place for the body would have been to bury it, although other rumours were rife that the body was dropped down a well which was then filled in. There were a number of wells in the area, as can be seen from the large scale maps.

I came across only one reference to any human remains having been found, that of Mr Searle in his account which appeared in the newsletter of the Beeston & District Local History Society in 1973 (see page 4), when he stated that his grandfather claimed to have been present when bones were unearthed in the orchard surrounding the Ash Flat House. We do not know the date when these remains were supposed to have been discovered, but Mr Searle's grandfather, Frederick Spray, died in 1910 at the age of 89. It is fairly evident, then, that this alleged discovery must have been made during the 19th century, and certainly before Robert Mellors printed his account in 1919 - and he made no mention of it. We must, therefore, be cautious in placing too much credence on this claim. Had human remains actually been found, it is likely that the coroner would have been informed, a proper investigation would have taken place and we would have expected the newspapers of the day to have carried reports.

Thomas Ballard, the last man known to have done business with the pedlar, stated that he (McQuince) intended to spend the night at the Ash Flat House. He might have done, but that doesn't prove he was murdered there. There was unquestionably some very strong circumstantial evidence to show that John Baguley had murdered McQuince, but it remained nothing more than that - circumstantial. In the absence of any material evidence - e.g. the body of the pedlar, with forensic proof as to the cause of death, I have no doubt that in today's climate, if John Baguley were brought to trial, a good barrister would have no difficulty in successfully defending him against a charge of murder.

Baguley could merely say that McQuince either didn't spend the night there, or that he did, and left the next morning. And what about Lee, who had the bad dream and walked over the hill to the Ash Flat House only to find Baguley 'digging an onion bed'. Well, that is exactly what he might have been doing.

But after the pedlar had disappeared, didn't the Baguley household suddenly appear much better off, with new pigs in the sty, and new dresses for the girls made out of the same material that McQuince had been selling? Possibly so, but Baguley could claim that he had purchased the material, possibly on credit, just like Ballard had done, intending to pay McQuince the next time he visited the area. And where did he get the money for the pigs? Well, he could say he had been saving up, or was at last using some of the £20 his father had left him in his will of 1793.

But then again, his first wife had made threats and said she 'could hang him any day'. Now, wives may say all sorts of things if they are angry with their husbands, and her comments can easily be dismissed as mere taunts in a domestic row. But wives could not testify against their husbands; and in any case, she was now dead.

And what about Baguley's reported death-bed confession that he actually had murdered the pedlar? Wasn't that, in itself, the most damning evidence of all? Perhaps, but can we really believe the possibly deranged rantings of a dying man, who may have been suffering from delusions? After all, he had claimed to see the pedlar in the corner of the bedroom, but nobody else present could do so, and his 'confession' might have owed more to the continuous insinuations and accusations which had been made been made against him over the years that he had murdered the pedlar, until in his dying days he actually began to believe them.

For every piece of circumstantial evidence pointing to John Baguley as a murderer, one can equally come up with a convincing explanation.

What do I think? Well, weighing up all the evidence I think that McQuince probably was murdered by Baguley and his body was buried somewhere near to the Ash Flat House. But as indicated above, one would probably have a hard job proving it. Unless, of course, one was able to get permission to start digging in the area where the Ghost House stood, but this would be difficult since the area has been much built over. It is interesting to speculate just what that might reveal!

And what about the haunting? Again, I am inclined to the view that the Ash Flat House probably was the scene of some unexplained poltergeist activity, but whether this was linked to a murder which might have taken place there I am not sure. Each reader must make up his or her own mind.

I can end this story in no better way than by repeating again the words of John Royston Pearson, the landlord of the Ghost House, who said, all those years ago, in answer to questions about the affair:

'I have given you the facts; you must draw your own conclusions.'

The following is a copy of the will of Joseph Baguley, the father of John Baguley.
(Courtesy of Nottinghamshire Archives Office, Ref. PRNW Nottm.1794)

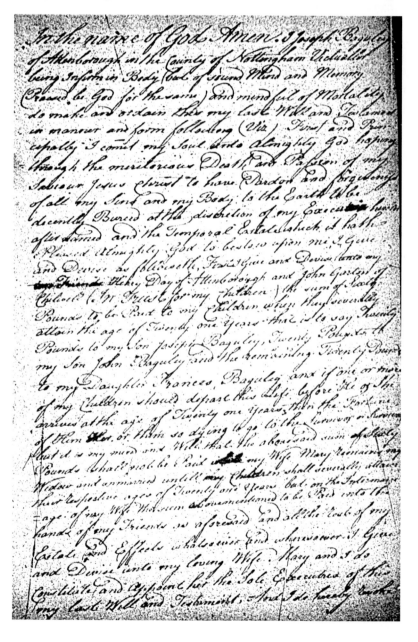

... and make void all former Wills by me at any time heretofore made. In Witness whereof I have hereunto set my Hand and Seal this seventh day of October in the year of our Lord one Thousand seven Hundred and ninety three

Signed Sealed Published and
Declared by the Testator as
his last Will and Testament
in the presence of us, and also
written too by us in the presence   Joseph Baguley
of the said Testator.

          John ✝ Lee
              his Mark

     Francis Baguley

Mary Baguley the widow Relict and sole Executrix named in the within written will of Joseph Baguley late of Attenborough in the County of Nottingham and diocese of york victualler deceased was duly sworn on the 8th Day of March 1794.

          Before me,

          Charles Coyte Surrogate.

     Pass'd 25th March 1794. 8.40.

65

APPENDIX B

CHRONOLOGY OF SIGNIFICANT DATES

The following is a chronology of the most significant events associated with the story of the Chilwell Ghost:

1788	John, son of Joseph and Mary Baguley, is born and is baptised at Attenborough Church on 29th June.
1793	John's father Joseph dies and is buried at Attenborough on 15th November. John is left £20 in his father's will.
1794	John's widowed mother, Mary, marries Henry Day, the Attenborough Parish Clerk, on 10th November.
1805	John Baguley marries Jane Maddock at Radcliffe-on-Soar Church on 17th December. He is aged 17, she is 21.
1805 - 1811	During this period, John and Jane move to Basford, where John works as a framework knitter.
1811	Diana and Maria, possibly twin daughters of John and Jane are born. They are baptised at Basford St. Leodegarius Church on 14th July.
1812	The Baguleys have now moved back to Chilwell from Basford. Maria dies and is buried at Attenborough on 14th June.
1814	Another daughter, Maria, is born and is baptised at Attenborough on 6th March.
1816	A son, Joseph, is born and is baptised at Attenborough on 1st September.
1819	Another daughter, Jane, is born and is baptised at Attenborough on 30th May.
1821	Another son, Benjamin, is born and is baptised at Attenborough on 18th September. John is now a labourer.

1827	Towards the end of this year the pedlar McQuince is last seen alive by Thomas Ballard. He is believed murdered and suspicion falls on John Baguley, inhabitant of the Ash Flat House.
1837	John's daughters Diana and Jane are sentenced at Nottingham Crown Court on 3rd November and are jailed for theft. The Baguley family is evicted from the Ash Flat House by Mr Pearson and moves to a house in Chilwell village. The Adcock family moves into the Ash Flat House.
1837/38	Over the winter of 1837/38 strange happenings are reported by the Adcock family. John Pearson attempts, without success, to find a rational explanation for the events.
1838 approx.	The Adcocks move out of the Ash Flat House and another family moves in. The haunting continues and this family moves out.
1841	Diana, aged 29, dies and is buried at Attenborough on 23rd May. She leaves two young illegitimate children. John's wife Jane dies aged 58 and is buried at Attenborough on 24th November.
1842	John's only surviving daughter Jane dies, aged 23, and is buried at Attenborough on 28th August.
1847	John Baguley marries a widow Mary Smith (nee Woolley) at Shardlow Register Office on 9th September.
1850	John Baguley dies, aged 61, on 8th February and is buried at Attenborough on 12th February. On his death-bed he confesses to having murdered the pedlar.
1892	The Ash Flat House and orchard are sold to William Hollingsworth.
1938 approx.	The Ghost House has an extension built and the Robbins family moves in. They rename it 'Sunnyside Cottage'.
1952/53	The Ghost House is demolished to make way for an extension of the Inham Nook housing estate.
1963	Building work starts on Field Lane and continues for the next few years. The whole area is soon completely built up.

THE BAGULEY FAMILY TREE

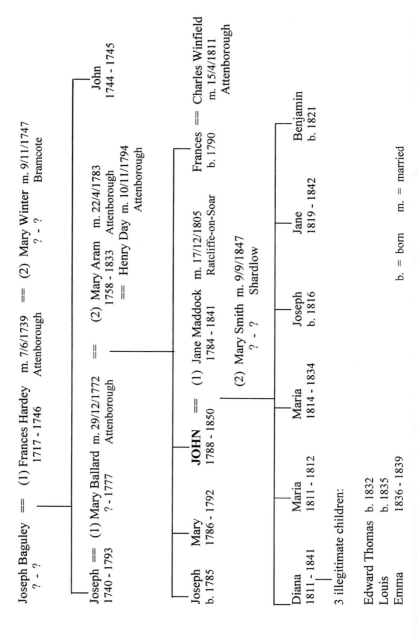

b. = born   m. = married

Narrow Marsh

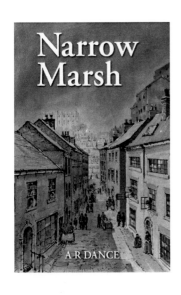

A R Dance

An exciting historical saga set in Nottingham in the early years of the 19th century

Nottingham, 1811 - a time of fear and hardship for the town's framework knitters. With low wages and long working hours, desperate men turn to direct action. And when a man is killed, someone has to pay the ultimate price. Young William Daniels witnesses the public execution, and from that day onwards he develops a burning desire for justice and freedom. But his chance encounter with the headstrong daughter of a wealthy factory owner sets in motion a tumultuous chain of events that will change his life forever. Set in early 19th century Nottingham, in an era of bitter social unrest, *Narrow Marsh* is a dramatic story of life, love and hope.

'One of the best novels I have read. The story just flew through my fingers and I couldn't turn the pages fast enough.'
East Midlands Arts

'A highly evocative story of early 19th century high and low life. At its heart, one of England's most notorious slums. Unputdownable.'
John Brunton, journalist and author

'The sense of overriding hope against unrest and misfortune will stay with you long after you finish this rewarding novel.'
Nottinghamshire Today

Narrow Marsh is published by Arundel Books
ISBN 978-0-9558133-0-6   Price £6.99

Available from all good book shops and **post-free** (UK only) direct from the publisher. Please send cheques payable to Arundel Books.

Leen Times

A R Dance

The dramatic sequel to Narrow Marsh

Having returned from exile in France, William Daniels has now settled in his home town and is developing a successful business as a canal carrier. But ever resourceful, and always looking to the future, he also becomes involved in plans to bring the railway to Nottingham. Meanwhile, in a penal colony in Van Diemen's Land, an old adversary of William waits patiently for the day when he will become a free man again. And as he waits, he carefully plans his revenge against the one whom he regards as responsible for his downfall. Nottingham in the 1820s and 1830s, an era of brutal change and fierce political upheaval, is the setting for this fast-moving story of retribution, radical politics and criminal conspiracies.

'Excellent story-telling. A fascinating marriage of fact and fiction.'
Andy Smart, Nottingham Post

'A thrilling sequel to *Narrow Marsh*, with as many twists and turns as the courts and alleys of 19th century Nottingham.' *Jean Boht, actress*

Leen Times is published by Arundel Books ISBN 978-0-9558133-1-3 Price £7.99
Available from all good book shops and **post-free** (UK only) direct from the publisher.
Please send cheques payable to Arundel Books.

Coming soon ..... ## The Westbrook Affair   **A R Dance**

Young Joseph Lambert has enjoyed all the childhood privileges befitting the son of a wealthy Yorkshire squire. But when his widowed father is mysteriously killed in a riding accident, his comfortable world is suddenly torn apart. Joseph's elder brother, the dissolute and self-indulgent Miles, inherits the estate and promptly abandons his young brother, leaving him to fend for himself. Determined to seek his fortune, the thirteen-year-old orphan makes his way to Sheffield where he secures an apprenticeship in a cutlery factory. Seven years later, now an accomplished craftsman, he marries Hannah and soon a daughter, Eliza, is born. But barely is Eliza old enough to know her father, when tragedy strikes. Hannah is struggling to support herself and her daughter, when one day an old lady arrives with an astonishing tale to tell. And slowly, a forgotten family secret begins to unfold. Set in Yorkshire and Nottinghamshire in the mid-19th century, *The Westbrook Affair* is a gripping story of poverty and wealth, betrayal and greed, and ultimately the search for justice and the truth.

The Westbrook Affair will be published by Arundel Books in 2012